The Graveyard Shift

Arizona's Historic and Haunted Cemeteries

Debe Branning

Printed in the United States of America

ISBN 13: 978-1-58581-046-8

2012 printing

American Traveler Press
5738 North Central Avenue
Phoenix, AZ 85012
800-521-9221
www.AmericanTravelerPress.com

Cover photo: Tombstone Cemetery courtesy Debe Branning
Cover and Interior Design: The Printed Page

Contents

Dedication

To all the pioneers who have left their legacies in the historic and haunted Arizona cemeteries...and to Kenton Moore, my partner in life and madcap adventures.

Preface

Arizona cemeteries are very different from the lavish cemeteries found in the Midwest or East coast cities of the United States. Although the early pioneers tried to maintain the cemetery lands with lavish plant life and trees, the lack of water flowing on to the grounds proved to be discouraging. Soon the Arizona pioneers resorted to planting simple mesquite trees, or varieties of aloe, yucca, and cacti plants.

Many of the early cemeteries fell in despair and were left unattended by families and owners of the grounds. Vandalism, erosion, and neglect turned the pioneer cemeteries into eyesores. Families moved their loved ones to newer facilities, or the tombstones were forgotten completely.

There has been a major shift to a growing interest of graveyards and cemeteries once again. Historians and preservationists are going the extra mile to locate old cemetery maps and records so they can chart the current grounds and keep an accurate inventory ledger. They are photographing each tombstone, documenting, and posting the information on the Internet.

With the popularity of tracing our roots through genealogy studies, knowing where our ancestors are buried has become important once again. Sometimes the simplest of tombstones will hold a vital clue to our bloodline or background history.

Cemeteries tell stories of disasters, plaques, and family tragedies. They also tell stories of love, honor, and accomplishments. Cemeteries were once thought as lovely parks where visitors could stroll down the lanes on Sunday afternoons to admire the artwork, and beauty of the tombstones. The closer your tombstone was to the pathway, the more influential and wealthy you were thought to be.

I ask you to punch the time clock, and get ready to go on the Graveyard Shift with me. We will travel to some of Arizona's most historical...and rumored to be haunted cemeteries. You will see cemeteries with well manicured lawns, tiny desert graveyards, tombstones built on the side of mountain paths, while others stand alone in remote areas. You are bound to learn a little bit about Arizona's history, and if you are really lucky, you might even encounter a ghost or two.

Cochise County

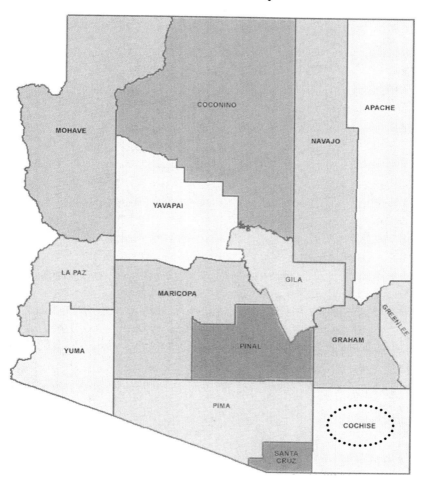

Ghosts of the Lost Castaways

Entrance to the 7th Street Cemetery

The Benson Pioneer Cemetery is also known as the 7th Street Cemetery. The land was deeded to the City of Benson as a cemetery by the Pacific Improvement Company; the California based land company of the Southern Pacific Railroad, in March 1929.

Burial plots were sold to residents by the City of Benson and the Cemetery continues to be maintained by the City. The first person buried was William McDonald, October 10, 1881. His grave is unmarked. The first marked grave is Charles H Fullerton, buried October 13, 1883. The last burial was Nicholas Solis in 1975. Some graves contain several bodies, as was common in old cemeteries.

The original map of the grave sites has been lost and a grass fire destroyed many markers. Surveys and updated information have been created through the diligent efforts of several volunteers.

Information was gathered from the Diocese of Tucson Archives, the LDS Family Center, and the descendents of those laid to rest in the historic cemetery.

Tombstone of Amelia Boak

But, the cemetery has a mysterious side to it as well. Almost everyone in Benson knows the story of Los Tiraditos or the Lost Castaways. In 1882 or 1883 Arizona was still a territory and there was not much in the way of law and order. Benson was a new railroad town. Although not as famous as some of the other towns in Cochise County, it had its share of gunslingers, gamblers, and thieves. A train was robbed by two bandits, and luckily they were captured almost immediately. About the same time, a horse thief was apprehended and brought to jail along with the train robbers. Three Mexican males were accused of these crimes. The story does no indicate whether a trial was held or not. The three men were hung for their wrongdoings on the main street of Benson. Ropes were thrown over beams inside or just outside the local stores and western justice was rendered.

The "upstanding" people of Benson decided that these men would not be allowed to be buried in the town cemetery since it was considered hallowed ground. Sadly, the three men were buried across a wash behind the cemetery in shallow graves marked with wooden crosses.

The Mexican members of the community felt these men were innocent. Over the years their lonely graves became a shrine to some of the town folk. Candles were lit and left near the mesquite trees across the wash. Bright crepe paper flowers were tenderly placed on the mounds. All Saints Day still finds Los Tiraditos cleaned and decorated. The three men and their burial sites are still separated from the historic cemetery by the eroding banks of the old wash. Some locals claim that late at night you can still hear moaning as the three souls plead for a resting place within the hallowed ground.

The lonely graves of the Los Tiraditos near the 7th Street Cemetery

A dove of peace adorns a grave at the 7th Street Cemetery

Directions:
7th Street Cemetery
South side of 7th Street
Benson, AZ 85602

Lost Boy of the First Bisbee Cemetery

I was in Bisbee, AZ to do another one of our Spirit Photo Workshops in 2004. We were staying at the Bisbee Grand Hotel and decided to do some exploring around town late at night. I walked the group up to City Park and explained how we were standing in the place that was once the Bisbee city cemetery. The old cemetery was closed in 1912 and the removal of the residents was completed in 1914. The city was sure all of the burials were moved—but because of incomplete records and decaying tombstones, one can only speculate a few gravesites were left behind. I spoke to the group on the sidewalk near the Bandshell staircase. I suddenly felt a spine tingling cold breeze rush through me. The hair on my arms stood up on end. I felt nauseous and dizzy. Other members of the group tried to stand in the same spot and felt strange, too.

The next morning I woke up with a horrible headache. I could barely function or think clearly. For the following three days I felt as if someone else was sharing my head and body. I was totally exhausted. Whenever I looked into a mirror, I saw someone else's face. Someone with a silly grin was over shadowing my own reflection. I could see it was a young lad in his early teens. He was not being malicious or disrespectful—he was merely using *my* energy and *my* eyes to marvel over the modern day world he never grew to see.

I met Fran Powers about twelve years ago when she was a writer with the local Bisbee newspaper, The Bisbee News. She spent the entire day following the MVD Ghostchasers team to and from every haunted hotel in Bisbee and wrote one of the very first media stories about the group. I had no clue she was seeing many of the spirits we were encountering and photographing that day. About six years ago she and I reconnected via email. We were now both authors of books on the paranormal and promised to get together to share ideas as soon as we could.

I purchased Fran's book, *Mi Reina, Don't Be Afraid*, and started reading about her life growing up as a budding medium in Bisbee. She has witnessed many unexplained events in her life time. Bisbee is a town is full of spirit energy and very haunted. I came to a chapter in her book that made me stop to read over and over again. It seemed that Fran had an encounter with the very same ghost boy I had met up with.

Debe Branning feels a chill as she encounters the spirit of a young boy on the grounds of the old Cemetery in Bisbee

In her book, Fran recalled bumping heads with a ghostly young lad as she walked past City Park on the way to her childhood home that overlooked the play ground. She writes that he was not a mischievous boy, but he certainly was bossy! She felt he was merely protecting hallowed ground. The boy would point to his mother's grave and try to explain it was blessed soil—not a place for the children to play. Lost in time, he did not understand the cemetery was gone and had been converted into a park and playground. Fran opted to avoid that particular staircase—and gravesite—at the park whenever possible.

Since Fran and I have reconnected, we have become very good

friends. I have even purchased a second home in Bisbee. It's almost like we have known each other from another life time. We both share the same passion for writing, preserving Bisbee's history, and still love a good ghost hunt. After my experience at City Park, and reading about Fran's encounter with the boy, I needed to know if this was indeed the same ghostly spirit.

Shiela, Fran and I walked up the 73 steps of the Bandshell staircase together. At the entrance to the park, I asked Fran to stand where she had seen the boy. She walked over and stood at the exact same spot where I had my own personal encounter. The three of us were amazed and excited at the same time.

Hundreds of graves dot the grounds of Evergreen Cemetery in Bisbee

I found a stick lying near by on the park grounds and placed it on the concrete where we had experienced our visit with the ghost boy in the past. "If you are here," I asked, "Please move this stick." We waited several minutes with my camcorder ready to film the boy should he show his presence. Suddenly, after all of our pleading and encouraging, the stick began to vibrate. We watched in awe as the stick wiggled and pulsated right before our eyes. And just as quickly as he made his presence known to us, he was gone again—back into the other dimension where the lost boy is eternally doomed to guard his mother's—and perhaps his own final resting place.

Directions:

In Bisbee, walk up Brewery Avenue to the Band Shell Staircase and up to the City Park.

Bisbee Ghosts Reunite At Evergreen Cemetery

Bisbee has long been the destination of dreamers, fortune seekers, and now paranormal investigators. In the early years, some of these prospectors left their families and friends on the eastern coast, traveled west, and arrived at the mining camps never to be seen or heard from again. Some met untimely deaths which left relatives seeking the mystery of their loved ones final resting place. This is a story of a man traveling through Bisbee in February 1912 searching for the ghost of his long lost friend.

For the melancholy pleasure of looking upon the grave of a departed comrade, R. D. Williams, a miner and prospector, made a search of various records in an effort to locate in Evergreen Cemetery the final resting place of a friend, George Savery, who died in Bisbee, Arizona in 1906.

The ornate entrance to Evergreen Cemetery

No record of the death and burial of Savery were found at the cemetery sexton's office and a search through the records of the undertaker of the city proved unavailing. Discouraged, Williams had almost concluded to give up the search. He had no other motive in finding the resting place of his friend, except to chant an eternal "Ave" to his soul, to repeat to the stillness:

> *Green be the earth above thee*
> *Friend of my better days;*
> *None know thee but to love thee,*
> *None named thee but to praise.*

According to Williams, Savery came to Bisbee after making a stake at Goldfield looking for an opportunity to invest. After being here only a few weeks, he became ill and died. With him at the time were two companions who had known him in Republic, Washington. They were Andy Clyde and John Sarofield and they saw their friend laid to rest in Evergreen and vanished to other fields.

Williams arrived in Bisbee and began an investigation to learn of the location of Savery's grave. If he could find Clyde and Sarofield, they could tell him where his friend lies in Evergreen, but to find them would be to canvas the four corners of the world.

"I just want to see George's grave," said Williams said in 1912, with a faraway look of longing in his eyes—true honest eyes that even yet light up with the friendships formed in the Klondike gold fields. "Many a time George and I marched over the frozen snow fields, dodged black coal balls falling in the mines, and endured all kinds of hardships. We traveled hundreds of miles through countless congers. We pulled our sledges from the back of our necks. I just want to find where he is buried and look on his grave. I would like to write to his sister and tell her that I had looked on George's grave."

Savery was also known as "Dugan" and it was possible that he may be remembered by that name rather than the name of Savery. It was possible that some of Bisbee's old timers may had remembered him or knew of the address of Andy Clyde or John Sarofield,

The Review offered to receive any information that could lead to the location of Savery's grave in Evergreen Cemetery. Perhaps the restless ghost of Williams still wanders the rows of tombstones in Evergreen still searching for the unmarked burial plot of his long lost friend.

Directions:
From Phoenix: Take I 10 East—take the 303 exit at Benson and follow HWY 80 south to Bisbee.

Directions to Evergreen Cemetery:
Go south from Old Bisbee past the pit mine. Turn east at Old Douglas Road. Cemetery will be on your left.

Ghost Lights at Fort Bowie Cemetery

Lonely graves of the Fort Bowie Post Cemetery

The Fort Bowie Post Cemetery is located in an isolated valley along the hiking trail that takes you up to the Fort Bowie ruins. A mountain called "Helen's Dome" over looks the historic cemetery. The post cemetery is evidence of the hard life at the isolated fort where the food was usually scarce, and the soldiers and their families shared limited medical aide.

The post cemetery actually predates the establishment of Fort Bowie. Soldiers of the California Column were interred here in 1862. The cemetery was unfenced until 1878. At that time, a four foot, double gated adobe wall was constructed to protect the graves from desecration by the post livestock. In early 1885, a picket fence replaced the adobe wall and the number of graves totaled about

70. By 1887, headstones replaced the weathered wooden headboards. Some of the headboards simply read: "Unknown. Killed by Apaches" The final burial was a murdered miner residing in one of the old officer's quarters about two years after the fort's closure.

The early headboards were simply pine boards painted white with cramped block letters in irregular lines. Those wooden markers have long disappeared, but thanks to Fort Bowie records and photographs, the cemetery has been reconstructed to represent its early image.

White headboards mark the pioneer graves at the Fort Bowie Post Cemetery

Five months after the fort's closure in 1895, the remains of 72 soldiers, dependents and "Unknowns" were removed to be reinterred at the San Francisco National Cemetery. Included were 40 identified and 13 unidentified burials, ranging in date from 1861 to 1892. It is thought that twenty-three to thirty-three civilian graves remain at the post cemetery site.

Of the most decorated burials was that of Medal of Honor recipient O. O. Spence. Also interred here were military dependents, civilian employees, Native Americans, emigrants, mail carriers, and three Apache children, one of which was Geronimo's two-year-old son.

Legends state that ghost lights are often seen in the fall and early winter whirling about the cemetery. The ghost lights are said to be the spirits of people who died at or near the Fort. The balls of light are usually blue or white in color. The rangers have heard the sound of horse hooves riding by the peaceful cemetery on quiet days.

IN MEMORY
of
LITTLE ROBE
Son of
GERONIMO
Apache Chief
Died Sept. 10, 1885
Age 2 Years

Top left: Tombstone of R W Wells

Top right: Grave marker of Little Robe—son of Geronimo

Left: Apache Chief Geronimo

One visitor to the fort in 1878 wrote: *"Knowing that persons now living have friends buried there, it may be a source of consolation to them to know that the graves of their departed friends at Camp Bowie are marked with slabs and that green grass grows upon every mound."*

Directions:

Access: The trailhead on Apache Pass Road can be reached from two directions: From Willcox, located on 1-10, drive 22 miles south on AZ 186 to the graded dirt road leading east into Apache Pass; From the town of Bowie, also on 1-10, drive south 12 miles on the partly paved road that leads directly into Apache Pass.

Fort Bowie National Historic Site
520-847-2500
Visitor Center is open daily 8am to 5pm
Except December 25
www.nps.gov/fobo/index.htm

Confederate Soliders at Dragoon Springs

Dragoon Springs was a stop on the Butterfield-Overland stage route that crossed its way through the Arizona Territory in pre Wells Fargo times. It is named for the Dragoon Mountains—which were named by the Third US Cavalry Dragoons who patrolled the area. It is located in the center of the Chiricahua Apache homeland and only a few miles from Cochise's Stronghold in the Dragoon Mountains. Dusty travelers riding west looked forward to this stop for a good warm meal, to quench their thirst, and to use of the facilities. The tired horses were fed and watered. Mail and supplies were picked up and delivered to the folks running the stage stop.

In 1858, the three men building the station were bludgeoned to death by Mexican laborers. Their graves and the graves of four soldiers killed by the Apaches can be found next to the well preserved stone foundation ruins of the stage stop. Although Arizona was still a territory, they seceded from the Union in March, 1861. It was during this period in time that a group of Confederate soldiers were assigned to gather stray cattle near the Butterfield Stage Station at Dragoon Springs. They ran into an Apache ambush and the Apache warriors killed four of the Confederate soldiers. These four men are the only known Confederate soldiers to have died in Arizona during the War Between the States.

The remains of the stone buildings are preserved and can be viewed by the public. The barren desert land surrounding the stage stop becomes a beautiful carpet of flowers in the spring time and offers a great photo opportunity.

Sometimes this eerie landmark becomes filled with unknown

spirits of the past. When the MVD Ghostchasers Spirit Photo Workshop crew was there in April 2006, many of the guests felt the presence of the slain solders. They seemed to be guarding the decaying stage stop and the surrounding area. The wind echoed strange cries in the valley, while whispers of another time followed us from the gravesite.

Graves of Confederate Soldiers near Dragoon

And, what is stranger, a phantom locomotive has been rumored to be seen and heard in the night by the residents of Dragoon and hundreds of other people. The ghost train makes its trek across the alkali flats of the plains between the Dragoons and the town of Wilcox. Some have seen its light and heard the engine and its whistle. A few of the phantom train watchers have been close enough to the engine to see a ghostly engineer pulling the whistle of the locomotive as it crossed in front of them. The trouble is, there never was a train that ran in the area…and there is no visible track.

Directions:
Take the Dragoon Road exit off of I-10. Following this road you will reach the town of Dragoon. Cross over the railroad tracks and the road curves to the right, but you will turn right off the paved road. Follow the dirt road around the northern edge of the Dragoon Mountains. You will see some Forest Service signs that will direct you to the site of the "Butterfield Overland Mail Stage Station".

Graves are located near the old Butterfield Stage Station near Dragoon

Four Confederate Soldiers were ambushed by Apache warriors near this site

Fairbank Ghost Town Cemetery

Fairbank was once the nearest train station to Tombstone, Arizona. Fairbank was the depot for the shipment of both cattle and ore arriving from Tombstone. Soon the town of Fairbank had a store, a saloon, an elegant hotel with a restaurant and bar, post office, several businesses and a schoolhouse.

Later the bustling metropolis sported a Wells Fargo office, five saloons, four stores, three restaurants, mill, and a much needed jail. For those travelers just passing through town, the Montezuma Hotel was constructed in 1889. The hotel stood just south of the Adobe Commercial Building. With every growing community a cemetery was needed to bury the unfortunate members of the town who met death due to disease, fire, murder and suicide. Fairbank's cemetery was a mere half mile out of the township, high upon a hill with views of the San Pedro River and panoramic mountains.

A wooden cross in Fairbank Cemetery

You can hike to the old Fairbank Cemetery. The half mile walk from the town center takes you on a pathway lined with mesquite trees and brush. It offers majestic views of the valley once you reach the hilltop. The graves in the cemetery are marked by piles of rocks and stones. A few weathered wooden crosses still distinguish some of the grave sites. Only a few of the burial sites have iron fencing protecting the early settler's final resting spot. The cemetery has an eerie, lonely feeling to it. Most of engraving or writing on the grave markers has faded into history.

Today the ghost town of Fairbank is the Bureau of Land Management regional headquarters and is part of the San Pedro River Riparian Area. The area is rich in natural history with remains of Pima Indian Villages and petroglyphs. Although Fairbank's main street is deserted today, many of its buildings still stand. The short, easy 1/2 mile hiking trail will take paranormal investigators to the Fairbank Cemetery atop a hill north of town. EVP has been recorded in the cemetery on quiet night with the full moon presiding over the graveyard. Whispers, shadows, and ghost lights are not uncommon during the vigils of paranormal investigations. Perhaps the whispers are only the ghosts yearning for loved ones to visit and lay fresh flowers on their graves.

Cemetery fencing and a fallen wooden marker
is all that remains at this gravesite

The one half mile journey to the cemetery is worth the hike

A crumbling cross lies in the desert cemetery of Fairbank

Directions:

From Phoenix: Travel east on I 10 to HWY 80 at Benson. Travel South to HWY 82. The ghost town of Fairbank is located ten miles west of Tombstone on AZ 82, east of the San Pedro River on the north side of the road. Follow trail signs to the Cemetery.

The Hunt for Johnny Ringo

Every now and then my paranormal team gets an itch to hit the road for a good old fashion road trip. You know...the kind of adventure that is planned about 30 minutes before you throw a change of clothes in a bag, grab your camera, fill the gas tank, and off you go!

And that is exactly what MVD Ghostchaser team member Shiela McCurdy and I did one Friday night after work. I grabbed my research files, hopped into her red Nissan truck, and we headed for Cochise Country. We decided to find a room in Tombstone since it's one of our favorite ghost hunting destinations in SE Arizona. We figured we could wander around haunted Allen Street after midnight and snap photos of restless spirits of the once booming mining town. But, as we drove past the Boot Hill Cemetery, we realized it was another one of those "Earp Holidays"—as I like to call them—and there was no way we were going to find a room. On to Bisbee, we decided!

We made the transformation through the Mule Pass "Time Tunnel" and cruised our way down Tombstone Canyon thinking we would easily find a room in Bisbee at one of the many haunted hotels or inns scattered along the mountain hillsides. Rounding the corner at Castle Rock, we saw dozens of motorcycles side by side in every parking lot. We shrugged our shoulders knowing there would be no room vacancies in this haunted city either.

Onward to the Gadsden Hotel in Douglas we headed. We knew the spirits would welcome us at the good old Gadsden. We ended up with a great room on the mezzanine. At midnight we wandered around the hotel in our PJ's and slippers with cameras in hand doing a little impromptu ghost hunt.

Johnny Ringo 1850 -1882

In the morning, I opened up my ever expanding research file and suggested that we take a little side trip and hunt for Johnny Ringo's grave. For several years I wrote letters, emailed Internet leads, and talked to local Cochise County residents as I feverishly sought clues to find the exact directions to the gravesite. For a long time it seemed to be a hushed, coveted secret. Nobody would divulge its mysterious location. With various maps and compiled directions we headed out of Douglas towards our haunted destination.

Soon we were heading down a dirt road looking for a ranch house on our left. I'd been told by many sources it was necessary to stop at the house to request permission to view Johnny Ringo's grave since it's situated on private property. We drove into the driveway slowly. It didn't seem like anyone was home, except the barking watch dog. We backed out to the road feeling disappointed. What could we do next? We pulled into a turn out along the road and made an amazing discovery. There was a worn path that led to a turnstile gate.

We grabbed our cameras and scurried out of the truck. We quickly followed the path to the unlocked gate and read a posted sign. "Please keep gate closed". Knowing visitors have been coming and going through the passageway frequently made us feel easier about not getting the suggested permission from the ranch owner. After securing the gate and ducking through a small grove of trees, we found what we had come to see—just 100 yards away was a lonely pile of stones nestled along the banks of Turkey Creek. It was Johnny Ringo's grave!

We felt greatly energized as we neared the grave. Still in awe,

Shiela and I snapped several photos of the grave and surrounding area. We sat down near the trickling waters of Turkey Creek to take in the serenity of the morning and pondered over the events that took place at this spot over one hundred years ago.

The gravesite of Johnny Ringo near Turkey Creek

The mystery surrounding Johnny Ringo's death has never been resolved. On July 14, 1882 Johnny Ringo was found dead in the crotch of a large oak tree along Turkey Creek with a bullet hole in his head. A coroner inquest was held and ruled his death a suicide. Some folks believe Wyatt Earp and Doc Holliday killed Ringo and made it look like a suicide. No one really knows the truth, but suicide still rules the official verdict.

It was one of the most surreal and mystical scenes a ghost hunter could experience. The soft breeze stirred the leaves in the aged trees, while the sound of the trickling stream made it seem as if the spirit of Johnny Ringo was in our company. Climbing back into the truck, we glanced down the path knowing we just encountered another component of the famed Earp saga.

We drove back to Tombstone and stopped at Big Nose Kate's Saloon for a cold sarsaparilla before heading back to Phoenix. We toasted Johnny Ringo's life and our successful road trip ghost hunt!

Directions:

Directions to Johnny Ringo's grave:

SW of Willcox, AZ on I-10 take Hwy 191 towards Douglas, AZ. At the junction with Hwy 181 (about 25 miles South of I-10) follow Hwy 181 for 12 miles to the Junction of Hwy 186. Continue East on a dirt road for 4 to 5 miles. Just prior to a house on left (North) is a turnstile. A path leads to the grave. Permission should be obtained from the house next to the path.

Phantoms of the Pirtlevlle Cemetery

One of the most haunted cemeteries in Arizona is the old Pirtleville Cemetery (aka Sacred Heart Cemetery) near Douglas, AZ. This small cemetery along Hwy 191 (formerly Hwy 666) is only a few miles from the US/Mexico border. Nearly all of its occupants are Hispanic. Burials no longer take place there at the request of the owner, the Diocese of Tucson. The cemetery is not plotted out in rows or lots. The graves were placed wherever there was a free space.

Most tombstones face to the east, but many of the markers in the Pirtleville Cemetery face South toward Mexico—so when resurrection took place, the person would go to Mexico. This unique arrangement of the cemetery was once featured in Ripley's Believe It or Not.

The MVD Ghostchasers paranormal team has visited the Pirtleville Cemetery on several occasions. One evening my daughter, Nikki, began walking from grave to grave spending several minutes meditating at each site.

"I can hear them talking," Nikki told us, "Some of them said "Hello". Others said "Hey," and for some reason I can hear water from a stream trickling past us."

I knew there were no rivers or streams in the nearby area—so I had no clue what she was talking about.

"They are saying they want me to stay here and visit the graves of the children", she added.

The rest of the night we filmed a glowing aura around Nikki's head. We have taken photos of the various tombstones with uncanny results. Certain graves and tombstones always reward us by displaying an array of ectoplasm, REAL energy orbs, and possible apparitions.

Mists, orbs, and other phenomena always
appears near this cross in the Pirtleville Cemetery

You will definitely feel the presence of spirits of the past lingering around as you wander through the cemetery of both elegant and homemade tombstones. One of our workshop groups received lessons in dowsing at the cemetery. We all experienced high energy around us, and it immediately made the fresh batteries in our cameras go dead.

And that running stream Nikki heard in the darkness of the night? The next day we drove back to the cemetery just after sunrise. We noted a dry riverbed that borders the south end of the cemetery. Pirtleville Cemetery seems to come back to life with phantoms and ghosts nightly.

"que en paz descanse"
(rest in peace)

It is believed that this is an apparition of
a young man in the Pirtleville Cemetery

Directions:
Pirtleville Cemetery is located on Hwy 191—8 miles north of the HWY 191- HWY 80 junction

Weary Willie and the Ghosts of Tombstone

From what we've been told, clowns can sometimes be scarier than tracking down a three headed ghost in a haunted crypt. Emmett Kelly Jr. was not that sort of clown. Son of circus clown, Emmett Kelly Sr., he followed in his father's clown shoes, and entertained generations of children and adults alike.

Emmett Kelly Jr, was born in Dyersburg, Tennessee on November 13, 1923. What some people may not know, Emmett was a Navy veteran who served in Okinawa and Iwo Jima in WWll. After the war, his father trained him in the art of clowning. He later donned the "Weary Willie" hobo clown costume and makeup. They say his clown smile was not as sad as his father's, and that made him an equally original icon.

World's Most Beloved Clown—
Emmett Kelly Jr as Weary Willie

Emmett collected model trains, but his true fantasy was his love of the West. In his later years he purchased a home overlooking the Wild West town of Tombstone, Arizona. Kelly did not know the house he purchased in the 1980's was haunted. Although he could not see the ghosts residing in his home, other guests did. However, he was able to experience the spirits by the fragrance of their perfume, and came home many evenings to the aroma of a fried chicken meal cooking in the kitchen only to find nothing there upon inspection.

Almost everyone in Tombstone knows the tale of the pelting pebbles up at the Kelly dwelling. Paranormal investigators, Kalyomi and Barb, wanted to learn more about the haunt, so they paid a visit to Kelly's daughter at the family residence in Tombstone. The two ladies stopped at the Kelly house early in the day, but nobody was home. Several hours later they ventured back and there was a truck in the side driveway with a man was standing behind it. Kalyomi could only see the top part of him—the bottom being block by the truck. They were both excited because someone was finally home. When she looked back, the man was no longer standing near the vehicle. They walked up to the front door and knocked. Kelly's daughter invited them in and they had some wonderful chats about the life of her father and the history of the house.

Kelly's daughter told them the house was built around 1892 and it is recognized by the pagoda style roof. It was owned by a man who once worked in the mines. Every day the miner walked home to find his wife waiting for him by the window. She was murdered in what was then the living room (now the front porch of the house), by a man who also worked at the mine. Their 4 1/2 daughter was also knifed to death.

When Emmett Kelly bought the house, he was a smoker. When ever he would go on the porch and light up, the pebbles started. It was a phenomenon that soon attracted not only his friends and townspeople, but people from all over the state. Family friends use to sit on the Kelly porch in the dark and chat. Suddenly they would be showered with 1/4 to 1/2 inch grey pebbles. They came from the ceiling, the living room wall, and sometimes from the driveway.

They believed it to be the little girl playing. The pebbles were never thrown hard, just sort of lobbed from out of the thin air.

Grave marker of Emmett Kelly Jr at the Southern Arizona Veteran's Memorial Cemetery

Emmitt Kelly Jr. stayed in the Cochise County area for the rest of his life. He died on November 29, 2006 just shortly after his 83rd birthday. He was buried with military honors in the Southern Arizona Veterans Memorial Cemetery in Sierra Vista, Arizona. Tombstone honors their legendary clown the second weekend in November with the annual Emmett Kelly Jr. Days.

Just a note: The man Barb and Kalyomi saw that day was not really there. Cherry Kelly was alone that day and had no company. She felt it was her dad paying a visit and hanging around his old truck that he loved so much!

Directions:
Southern Arizona Veterans Memorial Cemetery
1300 Buffalo Soldiers Trail
Sierra Vista, AZ 85635

Old Tombstone Cemetery

The Tombstone Cemetery has been the resting place of former residents of the "town too tough to die" since 1884. Tombstone citizens felt the need of a new cemetery where "proper" residents could be buried having met a feeling of status. Soon small wooden crosses were over shadowed by large granite, bronze and marble carved monuments. James Lamb was the first interment on June 30, 1884.

This is not the Boot Hill Cemetery where Tombstone's rowdy rogues and misfortune souls are buried under piles of stones. The Boot Hill Cemetery is full of history and visited by thousands of tourists each year.

Cemetery gate at the Old Tombstone Cemetery

The "new" Tombstone Cemetery, as it was called, is filled with ornately carved tombstones where visitors can read about the life of individuals who lived and loved in the once prosperous growing town. Many of Tombstone's founding families are buried at the large cemetery hidden and tucked away on the west end of Allen Street.

Tombstone Cemetery of West Allen Street

The cemetery is also known to be very haunted. One of most frequent reported events at the Tombstone Cemetery are glowing balls of light. Balls of light are commonly reported phenomena at many cemeteries around the country. This mysterious phenomenon is also known as will-o-the-wisp, spook lights, ghost lights, corpse candles or orbs. Some leading theorists believe the lights are the result of some kind of earthly geological occurrence that creates the ghostly flames. Others believe the balls of light that dance across the cemetery are the lost spirits of the dead—doomed to roam the earth for all eternity.

A MVD Ghostchasers Workshop found the crew in Tombstone and we were quite anxious to pay a call to the cemetery at midnight. With only the moon to guide us, we walked the dark lanes of the graveyard with tombstones flanking each side. Part of the group ventured to the back side of the cemetery where they saw a shadow move swiftly from grave to grave. The group sensed perhaps they disturbed someone's eternal sleep.

When visiting the Bird Cage Theatre, OK Corral, and other Tombstone attractions, add the Tombstone Cemetery to the list. It's historic—it's haunted—and it's FREE. For more Tombstone fun contact:

Tombstone Chamber of Commerce
www.tombstonechamber.com
City of Tombstone
www.cityoftombstone.com

Directions to Tombstone City Cemetery:

Head west on Allen Street and you will run into the Tombstone City Cemetery

Ed Schieffelin's Tombstone

Prospector Ed Schieffelin
1847-1897

In all the years I have traveled to Tombstone, Arizona, I had never taken the time to drive out to the monument erected in the honor of Ed Schieffelin. One Sunday, on the way home from Bisbee, I finally decided to take the side trip to visit the tombstone. Legend says Schieffelin was warned by friends, family and army scouts that the only rock he was going to find in the hillsides was his own tombstone. When Schieffelin discovered his silver mine claim in the hills, he decided to get the last laugh and called it "Tombstone."

Schieffelin seemed to appear out of nowhere in the desert. He had that wild, rugged prospector look that made people take notice. Sporting long brown hair and a beard, they say he had ghostly blue-grey eyes and a faraway stare. Schieffelin spent a lot of time in the hills near one of the area's most haunted locations, Brunckow Cabin. It is said he actually used the fireplace inside the adobe cabin to assay some of his ore samples after he made his discovery of the Tombstone mine. Schieffelin's second claim was ironically called "Graveyard."

After he finished mining his silver vein in Tombstone, Ed Schieffelin was itching to see the rest of the country and stake his claims elsewhere. He headed to the Yukon in 1883. When that expedition didn't provide great wealth, he headed back to San Francisco and married in the autumn of 1883.

Not one to stay in one place too long, the Schieffelin's traveled to Oregon to search the hills for yet another claim. In May 1897, a neighboring prospector found him lying dead in his cabin. Although he always looked much older in appearance, Ed Schieffelin was only 49 years old. The coroner reported Schiefflin died of heart failure.

Schieffelin kept a diary a good part of his life and a mystery surrounding his final claim was jotted down as his last entry in his journal. "Found at last. Richer than Tombstone ever hoped to be."

He was originally buried near the cabin in Oregon. But, when his wife went through his paperwork and will, she found another request he wished to have fulfilled. "It is my wish, if convenient, to be buried in the dress of a prospector, my old pick and canteen with me, on top of the granite hills about three miles westerly from the city of Tombstone Arizona, and a monument, such as prospectors build when locating a mining claim, be built over my graveyard or cemetery.

Shieffelin's Monument
near Tombstone

The mayor of Tombstone made the arrangements and Ed Schieffelin was finally laid to rest in his beloved Tombstone on Sunday, May 23, 1897. His wife, mother, brother and a large crowd of friends attended the service. He was buried wearing his old red, flannel shirt and faded prospector's clothes. Beside him they placed his pick, shovel, and the old canteen he had with him on the day he found his silver claim.

He would forever be known as the man who named the legendary city of Tombstone who would later be nicknamed as the "Town too tough to die." But it makes you wonder why Schieffelin selected this particular site as he final burial ground. Is his spirit protecting yet another one of his mining claims in the shadows of the Tombstone Mountains?

Directions:
To visit Schieffelin's Monument: Head 2.3 miles West on Allen Street and follow the signs.

Rex Allen and His Horse Koko

"The Arizona Cowboy" Rex Allen and the "Miracle Horse of the Movies," Koko

Rex Allen was born on a ranch close to Willcox, Arizona on December 31, 1920. At a young age, Rex discovered a love for music and received his first guitar. He enjoyed entertaining and would often go into town and play for tips in front of the barber shop. Rex Allen would grow to be a popular singer and actor known as "The Arizona Cowboy". When singing cowboys such as Gene Autry and Roy Rogers were all the rage in American westerns, Republic Pictures gave Allen a screen test and quickly put him under contract. Allen starred as himself in nineteen Hollywood western movies. He wrote and recorded several songs, many of which were featured in his films. His film career was cut short with the popularity of westerns fading by the mid 1950's. Rex Allen has the distinction of making the last singing movie western in 1954.

Rex's horse, KoKo, was known as "The Miracle Horse of the Movies." The handsome chocolate chestnut horse with white mane and tail was purchased at age ten from a Hollywood trainer. Allen fell in love with the horse the first time he saw him. When KoKo died, he was buried in Malibu Canyon on a small ranch owned by

Rex. Later Allen created a little park called the "Railroad Park" in Willcox. He had KoKo exhumed and re buried in Willcox. The memorial plaque at the grave reads "KoKo 1940-1967."

The larger than life bronze statue of Rex Allen was created by sculptor Buck McCain and dedicated in Railroad Park in 1991. On the chest of the statue is a molded heart with arteries symbolizing that Rex's heart will always be in his home town of Willcox. KoKo is buried at the foot of the statue representing that they will always be together.

Members of Cemetery Crawl 3 visited the grave of Rex Allen 1920-1999

Sadly, Rex Allen died on December 17, 1999. He requested his cremated ashes be scattered at Railroad Park where his faithful horse KoKo was buried. His presence is often felt in the park and the Rex Allen Museum by Willcox residents and visitors.

The Rex Allen Arizona Cowboy Museum and the Cowboy Hall of Fame is located in historic downtown Willcox. The building that displays the memorabilia of Rex Allen was once a tavern from 1897 to 1919. Now the former tavern houses spirits of another kind. A resident of Willcox was walking past the museum late one night when he heard one of Rex Allen's songs playing through the outdoors speakers. She believed it was Rex's way of letting the townsfolk know he is still around. A report of a ghostly cowboy has been seen in the museum leaning against Allen's old saddle on display. Most Willcox residents agree that it is only "Arizona's Cowboy" making a visit to his home town.

Directions:
Rex Allen Museum
150 N Railroad Avenue
Willcox, AZ
Museum Office: (520) 384-4583
www.rexallenmuseum.org

The Hunt for Warren Earp

Early portrait of Baxter Warren Earp 1855-1900

Baxter Warren Earp was born in Pella, Iowa on March 9, 1855. Imagine what it must have been like living in the shadows of his older notable brothers, Wyatt and Virgil Earp. He was far too young to take part in the Civil War as his older brothers James, Newton and Virgil did. He did, however, venture west to Tombstone, Arizona in 1880 and worked as a deputy for Virgil for a period of time, guarding prisoners, delivering papers and joining posses. It is not sure if he was in Tombstone during the Gunfight at the OK Corral, but he did not participate in that historic event. He did join Wyatt Earp and Doc Holliday on the Earp Vendetta Ride after the murder of older brother Morgan and attempted assassination of Virgil.

Warren left Arizona for a spell and returned sometime after 1891. He worked jobs as a mail stage driver and a range detective at the ranch of Henry Hooker. Warren developed a reputation of being a bully. He often felt it necessary to play off the reputation and notoriety of his older brothers.

On July 6, 1900 Warren Earp was having a few drinks in the establishment of the Headquarters' Saloon in Willcox, Arizona.

Hooker's range boss, Johnnie Boyett, was drinking in the saloon as well. Having been involved in several verbal confrontations before, the two men—both drunk—began to argue.

Entrance to the Wilcox Cemetery

Warren allegedly told Boyett to get his gun and they would settle the matter. Boyett left the bar and returned shortly with two Colt 45 handguns. Boyett called out Earp who entered from another doorway. Boyett fired two rounds, but missed Earp. Earp stepped outside of the saloon without producing a weapon. Boyett fired two more rounds, again missing his target. Earp entered the saloon once again. He told Boyett he was not armed and began walking toward Boyett, talking the whole time. Boyett warned him to halt. When Earp did not stop, Boyett fired off a fifth shot, striking Earp in the chest and killing him almost instantly. Boyett claimed he feared for his life and shot Earp in self defense. Warren Earp was found to be unarmed, but did have an open pocket knife in his fist. No arrest was made. The inquest jury's verdict stated Earp came to his death from a bullet fired from a gun in the hands of Johnny Boyett. Friday afternoon the remains of Earp were buried on a hill in the Pioneer Cemetery in Willcox.

Our hunt for the grave of Warren Earp began when it was decided the old Willcox Pioneer Cemetery would be featured on the MVD Ghostchasers' Cemetery Crawl 3 route in April 2008.

Stopping at the Rex Allen Museum, they were happy to direct us to the historic cemetery. We followed a dirt road for about 1/2 mile and came upon the entrance to the burial grounds. A drive around the small cemetery will take you right up to the grave.

Gravesite o f Warren Earp

The teams on Cemetery Crawl 3 said visiting the lonely grave of Warren Earp was one of the highlights of the weekend. They all slowed down to snap a photo of his resting place before racing on to the next cemetery on the road rally.

Directions:
If you go: From the Rex Allen Museum: Take Railroad Avenue and turn South on Stewart—drive about ½ mile—watch for Historic Cemetery sign on 3rd Avenue—turn left—follow dirt road for about ½ mile. Cemetery will be on your right.

Coconino County

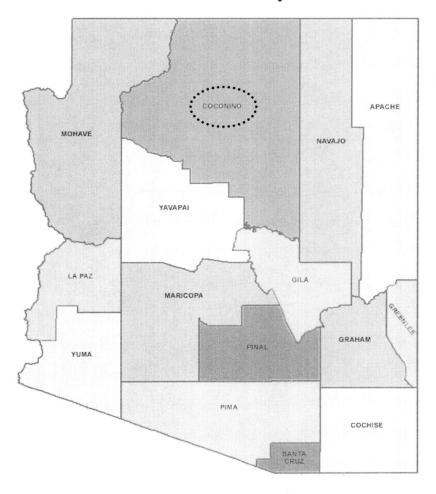

Flagstaff Citizen's Cemetery

The Flagstaff Citizen's Cemetery is the final resting place of many early Flagstaff pioneers. Several of the early gravesites face the north towards the towering San Francisco Peaks mountain range. The San Francisco Peaks are known by the natives to be a sacred mountain. The early pioneers learned quickly to tell the weather by simply observing the mountains. Perhaps the pioneer grave sites facing the northern mountain range are still keeping an eye on the beautiful Flagstaff weather. Winds, whispering through the tall pine trees, tend to make your visit a tad eerie.

A few figures of Arizona history have made this cemetery their final resting stop. From a sheriff who kept the lawless Arizona Territory under his order, to a mass grave to phantom flyers, and to a scientist who solved the mysteries of space. A walk in this cemetery offers a bit a déjà vous for all.

Commodore Perry Owens was born July 29, 1852 and died May 10, 1919. He was once the sheriff of Navajo County, Arizona. On September 4, 1887, Owens traveled to Holbrook, Arizona where he had a warrant to arrest an outlaw by the name of Andy Cooper. Cooper also

Lawman Commodore Perry Owens 1852-1919

went by the last name of Blevins, and was wanted in connection with the conflict of the Pleasant Valley War—a feud between the Graham and Tewksbury families. As Owens approached the Blevins house, the gang was already armed and ready for him. He knocked on the door and was immediately fired upon by its occupants. In just mere seconds, Commodore Perry Owens fired 5 shots killing Cooper, Sam Blevins, Mose Roberts, and wounding John Blevins. This gunfight has been noted in Arizona history to be as famous as the "Gunfight at the OK Corral" in Tombstone." Owens lived his later years in Seligman, AZ. He was laid to rest in a grave near the cemeteries roadways in Citizens Cemetery.

*Mass gravesite of TWA passengers
killed in a collision over the Grand Canyon*

On June 30, 1956, United Airlines flight 718 left the LA Airport en route to Chicago with 58 passengers aboard. About the same time, TWA flight 2 left LA and was heading to Kansas City with 70 passengers on the flight. Tragically, the two planes collided in midair over the Grand Canyon killing all 128 passengers. There have been many investigations and theories as to what happened that day, but the most likely explanation was the two pilots just did not see each other in time to avoid the collision due to weather, clouds and other distractions. Unidentified passengers on the United flight were buried in a mass grave in the Grand

Canyon Cemetery, while the unidentified passengers of the TWA flight were interred in a peaceful grave site here in the Flagstaff Citizens Cemetery

Gravesite of Vesto Melvin Slipher

Vesto Melvin Slipher born November 11, 1875, was an American Astronomer and the director of the Lowell Observatory in Flagstaff, Arizona from 1916 to 1952. He prepared spectrographs of the atmospheres of Saturn, Uranus and Jupiter. He photographed the planet Mars and was part of the team of scientists that discovered the planet Pluto in 1930. Slipher died November 8, 1969 and was buried in Citizens Cemetery in Flagstaff.

Listen to the pines…they will tell you where to walk.

Directions:
From Phoenix take I 17 North to Flagstaff. The Cemetery is located near the Northern University of Arizona campus.

Flagstaff Citizens Cemetery
1300 S. San Francisco Street
Flagstaff, AZ 86001
928-774-6725

Grand Canyon Pioneer Cemetery

The Grand Canyon Pioneer Cemetery is located on the South Rim of the Grand Canyon in Grand Canyon National Park, just a little west of the Shrine of Ages. The cemetery is maintained by the American Legion Grand Canyon Post #42 and is still in use today. Burials are limited to canyon residents who must meet certain qualifications and have permission of the Park Superintendent. To qualify, the individual must have lived at the Grand Canyon for no less than three years and must have made a substantial contribution to the development of, public knowledge about, understanding or appreciation for the Grand Canyon National Park.

Entrance to the Grand Canyon Pioneer Cemetery

Visitors to the Grand Canyon Pioneer Cemetery will find many familiar names among the tombstones that coincide with the Canyon's vast history. Some of these pioneer lived long lives at the Canyon, others lived or worked there for periods of time and kept a special piece of the area in their hearts. It is virtually a who's who of Grand Canyon history and contains roughly 304 burial plots.

Mass gravesite of United Airline passengers killed in a collision over the Grand Canyon

One of the gravestone memorials tells of the tragedy of the airline crash of June 30, 1956, 128 passengers and crew died then a TWA Constellation and a United Airlines DC-7 collided over the eastern part of the Grand Canyon. The planes both left Los Angels about the same time and were traveling east. They gradually came together at about 20,000 feet elevation. At the time, the accident was named the worst airline disaster on record and it incited the beginning of the Federal Aviation Authority. The remains of 29 passengers were never identified. They are lovingly buried in the Grand Canyon Cemetery.

Some of the other noted pioneers buried in the cemetery include:

John Hance: He was one of the first residents of the South Rim, prospector, and tour operator. Hance was known for telling tall tales and always had a interesting story about life in the Canyon. He died in Flagstaff, Arizona in 1919. His friends buried him in a secluded rustic spot about a mile east of the Grand Canyon Village. A few weeks later, Congress created the Grand Canyon National Park. The National park Service began a program of civic improvements and named John Hance's grave as the centerpiece of the first village cemetery. When you are there, take a look at his headstone and his footstone. Notice the distance? They placed the stones several feet apart as reference to John Hance's reputation for telling his humorous tall tales.

William Henry Ashurst: He was a Flagstaff resident and another one of the Canyon prospectors from the 1880's. He died in a landslide near the Colorado River below the Grand Canyon Village. Ashurst's friend, John Hance, buried him near the landslide. He was disinterred twice and finally buried in the Grand Canyon Cemetery.

The cemetery holds the remains of many canyon pioneers, park employees, and village residents who have passed on through the years, including Emery Kolb, Pete Berry, Ralph Cameron and early Park Superintendent M. R. Tillotson. William Wallace Bass has only a memorial monument next to his wife Ada. He chose for his ashes to be spread over the mystical Holy Grail Temple by airplane after his death in 1933.

Roy and Edna May Lemmons met when she worked at the Canyon as a Harvey Girl. At the end of the season, Edna was broken hearted when it was time to return to her home town. But, to Edna's surprise, Roy showed up on her doorstep on a spooky Halloween evening and they were soon married.

The cemetery is a quiet, restful, and visited by residents and visitors alike. Residents and others who have made important contributions to the history of the Grand Canyon National Park are invited to make this small cemetery their final resting place.

The Grand Canyon Park Rangers offer a October Cemetery Walk called the "Halloween Full Moon Walk" of the Grand Canyon Cemetery each year. Check this one of a kind tour on the fall schedule and learn a few ghostly tales of the canyon's secrets. No doubt there are a few of these former Grand Canyon pioneers still hiking to the depths of the canyon and back to the rim on a regular basis!

Directions:

The Grand Canyon Cemetery is located in Grand Canyon Village on the south rim of the Grand Canyon in Grand Canyon National Park, just west of the Shrine of the Ages.

Gila County

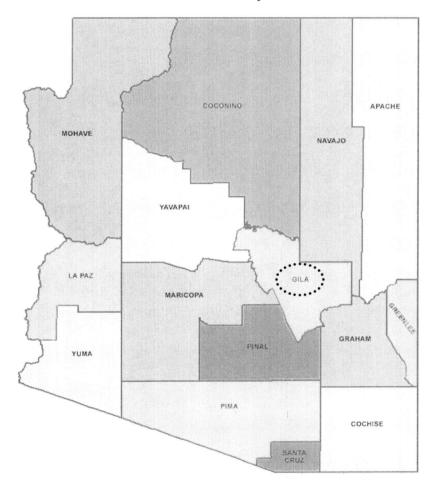

The Pinal Cemetery In Central Heights, Arizona

Entrance to the Pinal Cemetery in Central Heights, Arizona

The Pinal Cemetery in Central Heights, Arizona—near Globe—is actually one of four cemeteries in one location. Founded in 1916, the cemetery sits in a residential area built up around the final resting place of families living in the Miami, Claypool, Globe, and the Central Heights vicinity. The peaceful cemetery reaches flat ground to high atop of a hill dotted with trees and evergreens.

One of the most famous interments is of the notorious stagecoach bandit named Pearl Hart. Buried under her married name, many visitors to the cemetery walk right past the lady outlaw's grave without even knowing it. Pearl Hart has been nicknamed the "Bandit Queen" or "Lady Bandit" and her folk legend in Arizona has quite the history.

Born in Ontario Canada in 1876, Hart was relocated to Ohio with her family in 1878. Pearl married Frank Hart at a young age and bore him two children. Escaping an abusive marriage, Pearl headed west to Trinidad Colorado and arrived in Phoenix, Arizona in 1892. Frank Hart eventually caught up with Pearl and they lived a wild life on Washington Street in Phoenix. Frank is said to have gone off to the Spanish American War, and Pearl was left behind to get along as best as she could in the primitive desert town. Eventually, she sent her children back east to live with family.

The Lady Bandit
Pearl Hart 1876-1955

Pearl Hart took on the company of another rogue and together they robbed the Florence to Globe stagecoach. They were captured outside of Benson, Arizona and they were both jailed in Florence. The fact that Pearl was a woman bandit caused quite a sensation throughout Arizona. She was later moved to the Pima County Jail in Tucson. At sympathetic trustee helped Pearl escape, but they were both captured in New Mexico. She was placed on trial and sentenced to five years at the Territorial Prison in Yuma, Arizona in 1899.

Pearl Hart, prisoner #1559, was a popular folk legend and western dime novel writers often wrote exaggerated tales of her misadventures. Newspaper reporters visiting the prison often photographed Pearl posing with a six-shooter or Winchester rifle. Hart was pardoned from her sentence in 1902. After her release from prison, Pearl chose to live a quieter, and more private way of life. Turning over a new leaf, she met rancher, George Calvin Bywater, and became a dedicated rancher's wife for 50 years.

Gravesite of Pearl Hart AKA Pearl Bywater

Another Arizona legend buried in the quaint Pinal Cemetery is Chief Talkalai, an Apache Chief and Chief of Scouts. He was born in 1817 and raised on the San Carlos Reservation. Talkalai was the Chief of the Apache Peaks band of the Apache Tribe. He served as a scout for three US Army Generals. In April 1887, Talkalai was the leader of the scouts that marched into Mexico and captured Geronimo. He served twenty-one years as the Chief of Police on the reservation.

Chief Talkalai lived to be 113 years old

He saved the life of his friend John Clum—first Indian Agent at the San Carlos Reservation—and was forced to shoot his own brother. This deed angered his fellow tribesman and he was forced to flee the reservation and moved to Miami, Arizona. This popular gentleman mingled in the company of the Earp's, and president Cleveland and Coolidge. They say he died at the age of 113—the day the Coolidge Dam was dedicated. His tombstone is engraved with these words, "The White Man's Friend."

Talkalai's grave site is due north of Bywater's burial plot at the bottom of the hill.

The two Arizona legends from two hauntingly amazing walks of life have now met in a peaceful historical cemetery in the afterlife where shadows and balls of light float among the tombstones.

Directions:

Turn south off Hwy 60 onto Main Street, and continue to Golden Hill to reach the cemetery entrance. The grave site is approximately fifty yards NE of the flag pole.

Phineas Clanton and Pete Spence:
Partners In Life and Death

Pete Spence AKA Elliot Larkin Ferguson was a known stage coach robber and one of the suspected murderers of Morgan Earp. The gunfighter occasionally served the Old West as a lawman. He became friends with the Clanton family and rode with the notorious "cowboys." Spence once lived in Tombstone, and his house—which still stands today—sat directly across the street from the Earp's. Spence was also partners with Frank Stillwell on various business ventures—good and bad.

After the famous Gunfight at the OK Corral on October 26, 1881, the Clanton Gang took their revenge by orchestrating the murder of Morgan Earp. Both Stillwell and Pete Spence were named as suspects in his death. The indictment of Spence was eventually dropped, but that did not stop Earp on his vendetta ride of revenge. Spence turned himself in so that he could seek protection from wraith of the Earp's. He later committed manslaughter and spent prison time at the Yuma Territorial Prison in 1893. Pete Spence operated a goat ranch with his old friend Phin Clanton for a period of time. He lived out his later years in Globe, Arizona.

Although, Phineas Clanton was a member of the "cowboys" he seemed to be able to stay out of the limelight for the majority of his rough housing days. He was accused of being a part of the ambush shooting of Virgil Earp, but later released as there was no concrete evidence of his presence. He did serve a prison term at the Yuma Territorial Prison for cattle rustling.

Clanton returned to his ranch and married a widow named Mrs. Bohme and helped raise her 12 year old son, William. He became a respectable goat rancher near Globe, AZ, and stayed on the right side of the law. Phin was caught in a heavy snow storm in the hills near his home in 1905. He became ill and died in January 1905 from exposure. He was buried in the Globe Cemetery. At the time, his grave was enclosed by a heavy picket fence.

Grave marker of Phineas Clanton 1843-1905

Ironically, his good friend Pete Spence would return to Globe and eventually marry the widow Clanton in 1910. He died in Globe, Arizona in 1914 and was buried in the plot next to Phin Clanton. Both men, who rode together in life, are now buried side by side, together in death. They say at one time, Spence's grave was marked by a wooden cross. Weather and time decayed the tombstone, and there is no marker on his barren plot. Why wasn't a new marker erected at his grave? Why was a memorial gravesite and marker placed across the road? Which grave actually contains the remains of Pete Spence?

On a recent jaunt up to Globe, we decided to make a stop at the Globe Cemetery. We wanted to photograph some of the wonderful cemetery art scattered along the hillsides. I remembered to pack a set of dowsing rods in my bag and planned to conduct a little experiment at the grave sites of Clanton and Spence.

As a dowser, I wanted to solve this mystery once and for all! Was the gravesite next to Clanton occupied by Spence? Was there someone buried in the plot across the narrow road from Clanton's grave?

I took out the dowsing rods and waited for the breeze to fade. I stood at the foot of the plot indicating Spence was buried "somewhere in the vicinity" and held the dowsing rods in both hands facing forward. I asked the rods to cross as I walked over a body. I walked forward slowly over the top of the plot. The rods remained straight forward. I stood on top of the grass and raised the rod in my right hand high above my head. I asked the rods to indicate if a male or female rested in the grave. The rod remained neutral.

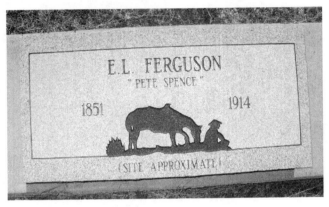

Memorial marker for Elliot L Ferguson AKA Pete Spence 1851-1914

Now, I began part two of the experiment. I stepped back across the road to the foot of the unmarked grave where Spence is allegedly buried. Holding both rods in my hands, I began to walk forward over the barren grave. This time the rods crossed as I walked over the body, and uncrossed as soon as I reached the top of the grave site. I backed up and stood on the center of the grave. This time when I held the single rod in the air, it slowly turned facing the foot of the grave indicating the person buried there was a male. We cannot prove that the body buried there is Pete Spence, but there is a good chance he is. The Globe Cemetery is a wonderful place to visit many of the historic lawmen and bad men of Arizona's History.

Entrance to the Globe City Cemetery

Directions:

If you go: Take l 60 East to the town of Globe. Watch for cemetery sign on your right. Turn right on Hackney Avenue and it will direct you to the City of Globe Cemetery

Graham County

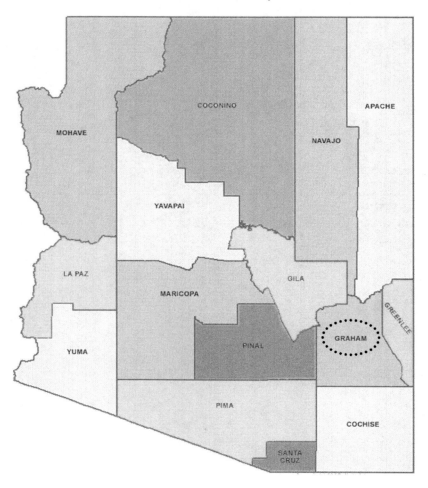

Arizona's Resurrection Mary

Entrance to the Safford City Cemetery

The Safford Union Cemetery is one of the oldest burial grounds in Safford and located at the rear portion of the Safford City Cemetery. The MVD Ghostchasers visited the historic section as part of Cemetery Crawl 3 in 2008. The tombstones are scattered over the hill leaving an eerie portrait of early Safford pioneers. Some of us have wondered what would happen if we were buried alive? This is a story from 1912 when a young girl's parents were convinced they buried their beloved daughter who was not yet deceased.

Mary was just 18 years old when she decided to end her life by taking ten grams of morphine. She lived with her parents near the old Hildreth ranch about eight miles south of Safford, Arizona. The girl had been sick for several days and very depressed over some matter that was worrying her. Her parents stated Mary had a fever the Friday afternoon she took the morphine that ended her life.

She was found in her room about 4PM in an unconscious condition and a doctor was summoned from near by Safford. When the physician arrived, he tried to resuscitate the girl, but the deadly poison had done its work too well. The suicide was undoubtedly planned by the girl. Mary had written a letter before taking the poison. In the letter she gave reasons for the act she was about to commit. Her depression was brought about by a love affair—a story of unrequited love.

The funeral took place the following Monday afternoon from her family home. The interment was to be made in Union Cemetery. Strangely, the life-like appearance of the body of the deceased girl created an impression that she was not dead. Examination before the burial Monday showed that mortification had set in and convinced the mourners that the girl was really dead. But, her family did not want to believe it—though they allowed the interment to take place.

The parent's doubt became so strong after the funeral that the father convinced several neighbors to go back to the cemetery on Wednesday to dig up Mary's body, which they did, and brought it back home once again. Another examination showed that mortification had *really* set in and to all appearance the girl was dead.

The great amount of poison taken by the girl had undoubtedly given the corpse the appearance of one being asleep, while all tests had proved that she was dead. The body remained at the home of the parents for quite some time as they did not want to give up the hope that she might come to life.

Mary was later laid to rest in a family plot in the Safford Union Cemetery.

Directions:
Safford City Cemetery
450 W Discovery Park Blvd
Safford, AZ 85546

La Paz County

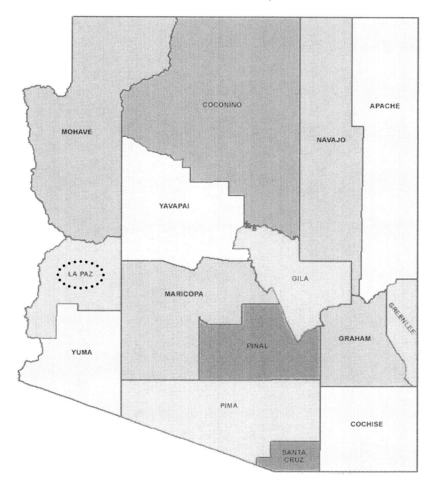

Eerie Ghosts of Ehrenberg Cemetery

Entrance to the Ehrenberg Cemetery

The town of Ehrenberg, Arizona was settled in the mid 1850's by Herman Ehrenberg. The town never grew to be very large, but by the 1870's the population was around 230 and hosted a hotel, and stage stop. It was also the landing dock for steamboats along the Colorado River with freight to be hauled over the barren desert to Prescott, Arizona. Not much remains of the original town today. With the addition of Interstate 10 and realignments of old US highways 60 and 95, the large stone pyramid monument marking the old pioneer cemetery is barely visible from the road.

Known as the Monument to the Unknown Dead, the significance of the old graveyard seemed to be lost on the agenda of most modern day travelers. Cross country travelers from another era sighted the lonely cemetery in the days when the two lane highway passed alongside it. They often chose to stop to explore and give the place a closer look. Some visitors were impressed by its history and the significance of the nameless mounds of rocks.

Old grave marker in the Ehrenberg Cemetery

Vandals carved names on to the old wooden headboards and monuments. Some tried to steal the tombstones in the unattended cemetery or scanned the soil in hopes of finding a lost relic or two. These days the Ehrenberg Chamber of Commerce is attempting to preserve and maintain the landmark cemetery.

Ehrenberg's boot hill was never anything very fancy. There are no humorous epitaphs, no monstrous tombstones, or souvenir shops near by like some boot hill graveyards around the country. Most of the tombstone markers in this cemetery are homemade weathered crosses and headboards. Every mound in the burial ground is there as a symbol of Ehrenberg's past pioneers and lonely travelers who died on the trail.

There has been rumored that ghosts are plenty in the old cemetery. Ghost lights have been spotted floating over tombstones and the spirit energy strong. Whispers, tobacco odors and orbs all have been captured after dark. Some witnesses have even spotted the ghost of a little girl dressed in Arizona territorial garb darting back and forth near the cemetery gates.

The cemetery dates to about 1862 with the last burial being in 1988. There are about 40 gravesites, most without markers. Wood crosses mark the remaining graves covered with stone. It is said that one grave contains the remains of a horse and its former ghostly rider.

Directions:
From Phoenix, take I-10 West and exit at Ehrenberg (Exit 1) and drive to the Ehrenberg—Parker Hwy. Turn left and proceed to the cemetery about one half mile on your left. Watch for flag pole.

Red Ghost and Hi Jolly

The plaque on Hi Jolly's Tomb speaks of a failed experiment in the Southwest desert long ago. It reads: "*A fair trial might have resulted in complete success.*" Jefferson Davis created what was thought as one of the greatest ideas of the 1850's. 'Why not use camels to transport freight and passengers across the barren southwest dessert?'

The US Calvary had 77 camels imported into the United States along with their Syrian caretaker and camel driver, Hadji Ali. Americans called him Hi Jolly. The Calvary team from the army posts soon found that the camels and Army mules did not work well together. And when the Civil War erupted, the plan was forced to be abandoned. The camels were either auctioned off or set free in the Arizona and California deserts to find food and water for themselves. Some of the camels were sold to the circus or zoos around the country. Hi Jolly kept a small herd of his own. He conducted a freight business between the Colorado River ports and the mines east of the waters. History records lose track of him from time to time, but they do show he lived in Tucson where he married and raised a family.

He later moved back to the Quartzite area where he mined and scouted for the US Government, delivered the "jackass" mail, and sold water to weary travelers. Hi Jolly reverted back to his given name Philip Tedro in his later years. Tedro died in December 1902 as he walked along the old desert road between the Colorado River and Wickenburg. He was 73 years old.

One legend said that Hi Jolly was still searching for one of his camels when he died. The story read that he found the lost camel during a sand storm and was discovered dead the next day with his arm across the beloved camel's neck. There are ghostly camp fire stories of Hi Jolly with several variations. One tale finds the man lost in the sand storm searching for Red Ghost—last of the camels. Variations of the yarn have the dead camel driver's skeletal figure tied to Red Ghost's saddle and doomed to ride the legendary animal in the desert forever more.

Graves dot the Quartsite Cemetery designed in the shape of a camel

A handsome10 foot tall pyramid tomb was erected over Tedro's gravesite in 1934. It is made from stones in the area such as petrified wood and gold quartz. Some of the stones feature petroglyphs on the exterior surfaces. At the top of the pyramid is a copper silhouette of a one humped camel that catches the glint of the sun as night falls. This symbolizes the legend of Red Ghost the camel.

The sealed vault at the base of the pyramid is said to contain some personal items of Hi Jolly. Legend also states it contains the ashes of Topsy, the last camel from the original herd. Topsy died in 1934 at the Garfield Zoo in Los Angeles at nearly 80 years old.

The MVD Ghostchasers and the ever popular Cemetery Crawl 4 made a stop this spring at the Quartzite Hi Jolly Cemetery. The group enjoyed the historical pioneer cemetery and a chance to learn the story about the Hi Jolly Monument. Several of the Crawlers took time to reflect and photograph the unique tombstone.

Newspapers report that to his dying day, Hi Jolly believed that a few of the camels still roamed the Arizona desert. He was right! The last wild camel in Arizona was captured in 1946. And the last sighting of a wild camel in North American was in Baja California in 1956. Some people believe the ghosts of Hi Jolly and his beloved herd of camels still ride across the arid sands of the Arizona southwestern desert...or are they just a mirage?

"Old timers down in Arizona tell you that it's true
That you can see Hi Jolly's ghost a-ridin' still
When the desert moon is bright, he comes ridin' into sight
Drivin' four and twenty camels over the hill"

Hi Jolly's Grave

Directions:
Hi Jolly's Tomb
W Main Street Quartzsite, AZ
Directions: I-10 exit 17 North side, about a half-mile east on Business I-10 W Main St. Turn north at the Hi Jolly Tomb sign to get to the Quartzsite town cemetery.

Maricopa County

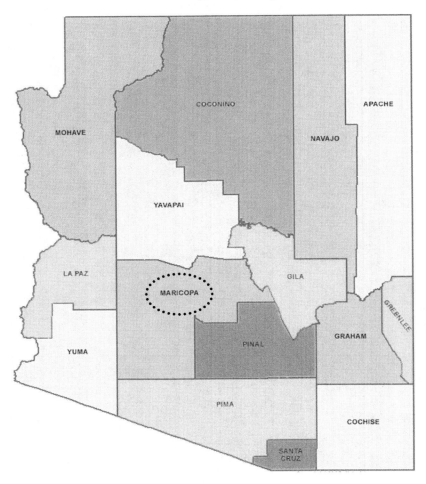

A Stroll Through Mesa Cemetery

Entrance to the Mesa City Cemetery

The Mesa Cemetery was first established in 1883 following a smallpox epidemic that claimed the lives of 44 residents of small community. As Mesa's population began to grow, more space was needed for the dearly departed. In 1891, land was purchased along Center Street—just north of Brown Road for this purpose.

Part of the original Mesa Cemetery was on the land where the Circle K at University and Center now stands. Clerks at the Circle K have noticed paranormal activity inside the convenient store from time to time. The graves of these early pioneers where moved to the historical section of the current Mesa Cemetery. Just north of the cemetery office is a section dedicated to "those persons unknown buried during the Great Depression." These folks were buried during a bleak period of time when permanent memorials were often a luxury.

An airbase was constructed in Mesa during World War II for training of United States and British fighter pilots. Over 2000 men were trained at Falcon Field, which today serves as Mesa's municipal airport. During the years as a training facility, 23 British cadets and one American pilot were killed in air accidents. These individuals are buried in a special section of the Mesa Cemetery.

There are several noted individuals buried in the cemetery including Waylon Jennings, the popular country western singer and songwriter; John Lee, a Wild West entertainer known as "Powder River Jack who popularized the American folk song, "Red River Valley"; Ernesto Miranda, whose 1966 Supreme Court case resulted in the "Miranda Rule"; Daniel W Jones, the leader of the first expedition party in 1877 to settle Mesa; and of course, Mesa's

Top left: Gravesite of Waylon Jennings is often adorned with flags and flowers

Top right: Country western singer Waylon Jennings

Bottom left: Gravesite of Ernesto Miranda

four founding fathers, Charles Crismon, Frances Pomeroy, Charles Robson, and George W Sirrine.

A stroll through the older section of the cemetery will take you to the final resting places of many of the pioneer families that have made Mesa the leading community it is today. There are many trees and the landscape offers a green park like setting for a comfortable stroll through Mesa's history. Long time residents tell me this was the place to hunt for ghosts back in the days when the gates to the cemetery were left unlocked after dark. They never knew what they were going to encounter during their late night games of hide and seek!

The peaceful grounds of Mesa Cemetery

Directions:

Download a Mesa Cemetery Walking Tour Guide
http://mesacemetery.com/pdf/WalkingTour_bro.pdf
Mesa Cemetery
1212 North Center Street
Mesa, AZ 85201
480-644-2335
http://mesacemetery.com/Home.aspx

Ghosts of the Pioneer and Military Memorial Park Cemetery

Amos J Randal: Died On the Job

As a volunteer of the Pioneers' Cemetery Association in Phoenix, Arizona and member of the Board of Directors of the group, people often ask me if it is creepy wandering around that old cemetery all alone. Are there ghosts? Do you ever feel like someone is watching you? Having to rake and do clean up around the old tombstones, I can honestly answer you, yes! There are ghosts in the old cemeteries.

Re enactor Mark Bradley tells the story of Randal's demise

One of my favorite ghosts in the old cemetery is Amos J. Randal. Randal was born in 1825 and was a native of New York.

He lived and worked for a period of time in the mines of South America—particularly Ecuador. He later lived in California where he enlisted and served Company A 4th California Infantry Regiment (California Column) during the Civil War.

After the Civil War, Amos and his lovely wife, Clara, settled in Prescott, Arizona and he was employed for several years in the undertaking business. The Randal's ended up in Phoenix where he became associated with Mr. Davis as *Randal and Davis Undertakers.*

One afternoon, Randal was preparing one of the dearly departed for burial. He was in the process of embalming a body of a gentleman who had been shot. Randal accidently stabbed his finger with an embalming needle. From that single incident, he suffered a case of blood poisoning on and off for about three years. The result of the original blood poisoning weakened his heart. Randal had another bout with the illness in September 1897, but during the weeks following he felt in excellent health. He was in cheerful spirits the entire day before he met his demise.

I guess you might say that Amos J. Randal died at his post. On the afternoon of December 1, 1897 he was standing in the Confederate Soldier's Cemetery, one of the many cemeteries that make up the Pioneer and Military Memorial Park. He had just finished overseeing the direction of a funeral. The body of G. A. Kirtley had been put in the ground, and the mourners were leaving the grave side.

Grave marker of Amos J Randal

Randal started walking slowly towards the horse drawn hearse. He had just untied the horse from his buggy when his knees suddenly gave way. He sank down on his knees, pitched forward, and fell on his face. Those that were near him ran to try and get him back up on his feet. Most everyone knew he was dying—or already dead.

The driver of the hearse, employed at Sturgis's livery stable, jumped into his buggy and drove rapidly into the city and notified the junior member of the firm, W. A. Davis. The doctor was summoned, but needed only a cursory examination to confirm he was dead. His heart had instantly failed him.

He left behind his dedicated wife, Clara, and four children Norena, Grant, Daisy and young Theodore. His funeral was held at the Presbyterian Church and he was buried in the Army Cemetery at the Pioneer & Military Memorial Park by the Grand Army Post. So when you drive past the group of old cemeteries after the midnight hour, keep your eyes peeled for the horse drawn hearse…and watch for the old undertaker in the top hat who may still be on the job digging graves in the darkness!

Directions:

Pioneer & Military Memorial Park
14th Avenue and Jefferson Street
Phoenix, AZ 85007
602-534-1262
www.azHistCemeteries.org

Ethel Kent: The Hunting Accident

*Re enactor Amy Westrick
tells the sad tale of
young Ethel Kent*

Miss Ethel M. Kent was born in August 1884 in the town of Socorro, New Mexico. She was the youngest child of Mr. and Mrs. Alexander J Kent. By the late 1890's, her family was living in Phoenix on a quiet neighborhood along north 4th Street. Sometime in 1900, Ethel was afflicted with a disease of the brain. This rendered an operation where they removed a section of her skull and they inserted a silver plate. For days she hovered between life and death—and her condition became so critical and fragile, that the slightest sudden movement might kill her. The street in front of the family home was closed and remained so until Ethel was pronounced out of danger. Miraculously, she recovered entirely and grew strong and vigorous.

After the operation on her skull, she became very susceptible to sever changes in the weather and particularly to the heat. In order to escape some of the hot weather in July, Ethel and her mother would leave Phoenix and join her father at another property he owned about sixty miles west of Congress on the Bill Williams

Fork. Her father met them in Congress and the journey they made to the mine was made without incident.

Two men who had been hunting pigeons came to the Kent camp to visit. One of the men leaned a gun against a rock some little distance from where the family was sitting. In some uncountable manner—for no one was near it—the gun fell to the ground, discharged, and severely wounded Ethel in the foot. It tore away the greater part of her foot and she was bleeding heavily. The family packed up and started for Congress at once as medical aid could not be obtained any place nearer. The accident happened about 7:00 in the evening and it was nearly 10:00 the following night before the horrified Kent's reached Congress.

A plain wooden headboard marks the grave of Ethel Kent

The heat was intense, the water was scant, and the quality of the water was bad. Even with the hygienic tablets to retard stagnation, it was hardly fit to drink. Once they arrived in Congress, Ethel was given medical attention, but her terrible wound—together with the intense heat of the desert had zapped her strength and she died at 8:30 the following day, July 18, 1901. Her grief stricken parents brought Ethel back to Phoenix on the train.

They held Ethel's funeral at her parent's home. There was a large attendance of sorrowing friends and the pall bearers were members of the Epworth League (Methodist Episcopal church youth organization) an organization which she had been an earnest and faithful worker. Ethel was only 15 years old—almost

16. She had so much to look forward to. A white wooden board marks her burial in the Masonic Cemetery.

Directions:
Pioneers' Cemetery Association
Pioneer & Military Memorial Park
14th Avenue and Jefferson Street
Phoenix, AZ 85007
602-262-6412
www.azHistCemeteries.org

Frank B Moss: Acute Indigestion

I have mentioned the area of Central and Washington before as a potential haunted location in downtown Phoenix, Arizona. Once the heart of the territorial city, it was also a center of death, murder, and suicides. The area has changed through the years, but it still carries high energy with Chase Field, and US Airways Center at the current locale. This same area also houses museums and convention centers. At times you may experience a sense of déjà vu as you go about your business.

The original Phoenix City Hall was located on Washington and Central and sat in the area where the downtown bus terminal stood until recently. Built in 1888, the building served the city up into the 1920's when a more modern facility was built on 125 West Washington.

Frank B Moss 1852-1906

Frank B Moss was the acting Mayor of Phoenix in 1906. He was born in Wisconsin in 1852. His father was a blacksmith and he followed in his father's footsteps by opening his own blacksmith shop on 4th Avenue between Washington and Jefferson Streets. He later became the Phoenix fire chief and was a strict Republican.

On March 22, 1906, Moss felt very sick to his stomach. He had vomited in the streets and was embarrassed that citizens would think he had been drinking. He had not touched a drop of liquor in several years. Between 7 and 8PM he arrived at City Hall. He placed his bicycle on the rack and ascended the City Hall stairs. He started to go through the entrance to the building. He stumbled and asked the guard if he would please call a doctor. The physician arrived and administered some stomach medications and told him to lie down on a cot in a back room. When they checked on Frank Moss between 9 and 10PM, he had no pulse. Moss had died at City Hall. There was no evidence of poison. His death certificate read he died of acute indigestion which induced a heart clot.

Re enactor Robert Everson tells the tale of the Mayor's last day in office

His funeral was held in the council chamber of the City Hall. He lay in the grand hallway at the main entrance. American flags, potted plants, greenery and a draping of black were the backdrop of this solemn occasion. Every store and shop on Washington closed from 1:30 to 4PM during the funeral service. Even the street cars stopped running. The funeral cortege was led by the Pioneer Band as they headed to the IOOF section of the old pioneer Cemetery.

If you are walking to nearby establishments for a few more drinks and food after the big game, remember your Tums. Too many hot dogs and nachos could lead you to a close encounter with the former Mayor's ghost who unfortunately over indulged in his eating pleasures as well.

Grave of Frank B Moss

Directions:

Pioneers' Cemetery Association
Pioneer & Military Memorial Park
14th Avenue and Jefferson Street
Phoenix, AZ 85007
602-262-6412
www.azHistCemeteries.org

Henry Garfias: Capture of the Ghost Bandit

Henry Garfias was born in California and came to Wickenburg, Arizona in 1871. He relocated to Phoenix and became a peace officer in 1874. In the early days when outlaws were plentiful, he was appointed as the city marshal. Due to his nerve, judgment and unerring aim, Garfias kept Phoenix protected from members of the rough element. Although he was small in stature, he was a giant in strength and knew no word as fear.

In 1881, Garfias was named a deputy to Maricopa County Sheriff Lindley H. Orme. He was sent on a special assignment to Gillette, a small mining town north of Phoenix along the Agua Fria River, to solve the mystery of the Ghost Bandit.

Henry Garfias sits with other lawmen at the Phoenix Police Office

The mysterious Ghost Bandit was a crafty highwayman who robbed the Black Canyon Stage Coach three times in just a few weeks, taking $20,000, $26,000 and $22,000 of the mine payroll money. The elusive Ghost Bandit appeared after dark. He always materialized from behind the rocks along the side of the road where it cross the Aqua Fria River. The phantom robber carried a rifle, wore a colorful bandana for a mask, and never left any trace of footprints behind. There were no horse hoof prints or signs of physical presence.

Garfias gathered the concerned people of Gillette together and tried to unravel the mystery. Then he spoke to the young children of the Mexican miners. A few of the boys told him that on the day of the last robbery, the blacksmith, Henry Seymour, had set out to go rabbit hunting with his rifle. The sharp young lads also noticed that Seymour was carrying several gunny sacks under his arm.

Re enactor Gary Tone tells the story of Henry Garfias and the Ghost Bandit

The deputy lawman planned carefully and decided to bait a trap. He happened to mention to Henry Seymour that the Black Canyon Stage would be carrying a bonanza of a pay load on a certain day. Garfias hid out in the Aqua Fria crossing waiting for Seymour. Just as planned, Seymour arrived with his feet wrapped in gunny sacks waiting to overtake the stage driver. Garfias appeared from hiding and stuck a six gun in the Ghost Bandit's ribs. Seymour was arrested and carted off to jail.

Seymour received ten years in prison for his 'ghostly' deeds, but refused to confess where he had hidden the $67,000. Most likely the loot is still buried somewhere in the vicinity of Gillette. There might still be a "ghost of a chance" we paranormal investigators could recover the loot. Dowsing rods, anybody?

Directions:

Pioneers' Cemetery Association
Pioneer & Military Memorial Park
14th Avenue and Jefferson Street
Phoenix, AZ 85007
602-262-6412
www.azHistCemeteries.org

Letitia Rice: Scorned and Burned

Long ago when Phoenix was just a new territory city, it had its share of saloons and brothels just like its neighboring Arizona mining towns. Where office buildings and hotels stand in downtown Phoenix today, you are witnessing the stomping grounds of the pioneers of Phoenix. The next time you are standing in a building near Van Buren and 1st Street, and feeling a ghostly presence or two, it might be because of some of the violence that took place in other establishments located on the grounds. You see, there once stood a house of prostitution at that location, and back in 1893, one of the girls met her untimely death at that spot!

Tessie was merely 17 years old in May of 1893. She was a working girl and employed by madam Minnie Powers at her house of prostitution on Van Buren. Ms Powers had left for the evening for a night at the theater. And while the cat is away, the mice in the "cat house" will play. Tessie and another one of the girls, Ruth, decided to go on a wild buggy ride with a few of the gentlemen callers.

Re enactor Cammielle Becker
tells about the horrifying fire
that burned Leticia Rice

After a night of carousing and drinking, the party ended back at the house. Tessie was more than a little tipsy and was very defiant about going back into the brothel. The gentlemen were forced to carry her into the house and down to her room. The whole time Tessie was kicking and screaming not wanting to end her drunken spree. In the scuffle, she accidently knocked over a lamp from a small table stand. Striking the floor, the lamp exploded.

The explosion spewed coal oil in the hair of one of the girls preparing the bed in Tessie's room. Unfortunately for Tessie, the fire from the explosion burned this once beautiful girl from her head to her knees. The gentlemen, not wanting *their* reputations tarnished for being inside this house of repute, fled the scene. The ladies of the house, however, acted fast. One of the girls snuffed out the flames on Tessie and the carpeted floor with old clothing while another managed to drag the hose into the house to extinguish any remaining embers.

Poor Tessie was placed on a bed and the doctor was summoned. With her parched face all blackened and cracked by the heat, there was not much anyone could do. Her charred face and stomach presented a ghastly spectacle. Her nose had been burned away. Tessie died later in the day from inhaling the fire which resulted in shock from the burns.

Tessie's mother in El Paso was telegraphed. They contacted her sisters in Globe and Tombstone, who may have been working as soiled doves too. Another sister in Bisbee, AZ died just a few weeks earlier. Tessie was known by many names—Blanche Russell, Tessie Murray, Mrs. C. W. Wright—but the name she is buried under is Letitia B Rice. A plot in Loosley Cemetery was donated to her and her simple tombstone reads:

Letitia Rice
17 yr 1 mo 24 days
Gone but not forgotten

Gravestone of Letitia Rice

And now you know why you have felt a little extra warm as you stood on Van Buren and 1st Streets…and it's not just because "it's a dry heat."

Directions:

Pioneers' Cemetery Association
Pioneer & Military Memorial Park
14th Avenue and Jefferson Street
Phoenix, AZ 85007
602-262-6412
www.azHistCemeteries.org

Martha Beatty: All Washed Up

Martha Beatty was one of the early Phoenix, Arizona residents. She was born in Pennsylvania in August 1829. She married Benjamin Beatty, who was a merchant and they had one child. Daughter, Sarah, was born in 1848. From the 1850's through the 1880's, the Beatty's owned a lovely home in the Midwest state of Iowa.

In 1900, at the age of 70, Martha was a pioneer living in the Arizona Territory in the town of Phoenix. She arrived in the valley in 1894 from Eddyville Iowa. Martha relocated to Arizona for health reasons. Mrs. Beatty, now a widow, had no relatives in Arizona. She lived in a cozy home near the park and the streetcar barns.

Gravestone of Martha Beatty

Martha was 73 years old in 1902 and suffered from a bout of consumption. She was getting very weak in her old age. Her long time neighbor, Mrs. Conley, kindly offered to look after her. She often helped with her baths at the Frank Shirley "tonsorial parlors" (barber shop) in the basement of the Goodman Drug Store. The bath house was located at the corner of Washington and Center Streets. (Now Central Avenue)

Mrs. Conley was called to meet Mrs. Beatty at 1PM at tonsorial parlor to assist with giving Martha her bath. Being old and feeble, it was not easy for her to bathe on her own. Unfortunately, Mrs. Conley did not arrive to the bath house until 2PM. They found Martha in the tub lying on her side with her face covered with water. The water was running over the edge of the tub and on to the floor. They lifted Martha from the tub and laid her on the floor of the bath house. Dr. Plath was summoned, but she had already died by the time he arrived. Martha Beatty had fainted from the extreme heat of the water and drowned.

Her funeral was held at the near by undertaking parlor and she was laid to rest in Rosedale Cemetery where she could bathe in the eternal sunshine. A lot of interest was sparked when her will and testament was read. For years she had asked her relatives in Lincoln, Iowa to come to Arizona and help nurse and take care of her. None of them bothered to answer her pleas. To their dismay, she bequeathed her entire estate of $3,293.50 to Lincoln University in Iowa. Let that be a lesson to them!

Historic graves and crypts dot the grounds of Rosedale Cemetery

---

Directions:
Pioneer & Military Memorial Park
14th Avenue and Jefferson Streets
Phoenix AZ 85007
602-534-1262
pioneercem@yahoo.com
www.azHistCemeteries.org

Phantom Flasher of the Old Cemetery

We all know that the month of July in Phoenix, Arizona can be unbearably hot. It even doubles the discomfort zone when the humid monsoons begin to set in. Back in July 1912, a few Phoenix women had an encounter in the middle of the night with what might have been a ghost!

A mysterious man was seen by three women who lived on West Jefferson Street just opposite of the home of Deputy Wilson. To keep cool, the women slept on cots in the front yard, wrapped in damp bed sheets, near the sidewalk. In the early days of Phoenix, it was a common practice to sleep on open aired porches, or line cots on the lawns in order to get a comfortable nights sleep during the hot muggy weather.

About 1:30am, one of the women saw a man walking along the sidewalk and stopped within a few feet of her cot. He was a white man, rather heavy-set, and was as innocent of clothing as a new born baby.

A piercing scream by the woman woke the neighborhood, but it did not seem to disturb the mysterious stranger in the night. He simply walked west to the corner and turned south toward the graveyard. Both of the other two women saw him "disappear."

The woman roused Deputy Wilson who made a search for the naked stranger. He could obtain no trace of him, however, and finally the women gained courage enough to return to their home. In the morning, Wilson tracked the man to the graveyard and out to the hard ground to the southwest. It was easy enough to track him until the ground became extremely dry and packed. The prints of his bare feet simply vanished in the old cemetery.

Wilson telephoned the asylum later in the morning and was told that no patient had escaped the institution. Was this a peeping Tom, or one of the dead from the cemetery taking a moonlight stroll in the "dead hours" of the night?

Kittie Quackinbush

Linville Family plot

Directions:
Pioneer & Military Memorial Park
14th Avenue and Jefferson Street
Phoenix, AZ 85007
602-534-1262
www.azhistcemeteries.org

Volunteers of the Pioneer's Cemetery Association
prepare for the annual Memorial Day event

"Red" Nelson: Deflated Balloon

During the past several years I have talked to many Phoenix—or former Phoenix residents that have grown up in areas that seemed to have more paranormal activity than others. The downtown area of Phoenix which was the original settlement of the city is one of those sites where apparitions and ghostly happenings seem consistent. As a paranormal investigator and a historian, I am always running into mind boggling stories as I read the old newspapers. Today I would like to share one of those stories about downtown Phoenix and let you wonder if this is one of the specters Phoenicians see standing outside their windows or wandering in a daze through their property.

Do you think one has more of a chance of becoming a ghost if Karma or the stars are lined up predicting a disaster? Take the case of W. H. 'Red' Nelson who on August 1, 1895 became a victim of an accident nobody would ever have predicted...or would they?

Nelson was born in York, PA, was unmarried and traveling with his business partner, Otto Burke, a hot air balloonist or aeronaut as they were called in the day. He was about 35 years old. They started from San Francisco early in June on their performance circuit and expected to work through TX before returning to the coast. Otto Burke and "Professor" Nelson were great entertainers and professional balloonists.

Their act showcased a colorful hot air balloon that tugged at the ropes tethering it to a solid surface. One of them would grip the dangling rope tied to the trapeze bar suspended from lines attached to the balloon's netting. Hand over hand they climbed the rope and mounted the bar. At their signal the tethers were cut, and the balloon began its steady ascent. They performed a trapeze act as the gas-filled orb rose to perilous height. At more than 1,000 feet above the ground, the aeronaut jumped from the bar and hurled earthward at dizzying speed. Then his parachute opened, and he slowly and gracefully dropped to earth.

On the afternoon of August 1, 1895 a crowd gathered at the once vacant lot on South Center Street (now Central Avenue) to watch the balloon ascension. By the middle of the afternoon hundreds were crowded around the merry-go-round and gospel tent. The big balloon—fifty feet high and thirty feet in diameter was inflated—took off around 5:30pm. Otto Burke was operating the balloon for the first launch. The end of the balloon pulled out leaving a hole about eight feet in diameter. The balloon collapsed as the gas escaped and landed on the sheds of a near by lumber company. Burke fell about 30 feet. He was considerably bruised but not seriously injured.

Trapeze shows off a tethered hot air balloon
that was big entertainment in 1895

There seemed to be a feeling of disappointment as most of the crowd had come from the country to witness the ascension, yet nobody could be blamed for the deflated balloon and the accident. The balloon had seen much active service and had grown unsafe.

Re enactor Robert Everson talks about "Red" Nelson's last aeronaut stunt

The balloon was inflated a second time and 7:15 "Red" Nelson went to the trapeze bar and perhaps gave his last perilous and foolhardy exhibition. As the balloon shot up, a strong SE breeze was blowing; the near full moon was partly hidden by a cloud. Nelson applied the knife to the cutaway rope. It was also observed that the parachute opened up and everyone on the ground thought the ascent was a success. The parachute descended over the house of Joseph Thalheimer. Thalheimer stated that he and his family were at dinner at the time when he suddenly heard a crash on the roof, and then something rolled off the roof in his back yard where he found the body of Nelson with his right hand still clinging to the trapeze bar of the parachute. The parachute had fallen on another building half a block away. If it was lifted by the light breeze that far after Nelson cut loose the bar, he must have separated from it at a dizzy height. He must have been tired for he had worked all day about the balloon and only undertook the perilous ascent after his partner was injured. He wanted to prove to the unreasonable and heartless persons in the crowd that the show was no fake.

Not a bone was broken, but there were bruises over half his body. There was an ugly cut on his jaw and another near the left eye. The tissues were so thoroughly crushed that the undertaker was hardly able to find a vein to inject the embalming fluid.

Now here is where the superstition theories fall into the story. The most plausible theory of the time was that the lot where the performance took place was on consecrated ground, having for more than a year been the scene of a nightly meeting of the Salvation Army. True, the merry-go round had disputed rights in the premises, and on August 1st, it was gathering in many nickels that might otherwise have dropped in the collection box. At any rate, Satan was the blame for the outcome of this occasion. As unfortunate as it was that no trapeze performance in mid-air was witnessed by the assembled throng, there were those present that felt the disaster was only just retributive justice meted out to the trespassers on sacred ground.

Burke and Nelson came to Arizona in June of 1895 and then to Phoenix some time in July. They were persistently pursued by bad luck, and it may interest you superstitious folks to learn that Nelson's last and fatal ascent was his *thirteenth!*

The funeral expenses were paid by the merry go round proprietor whose place the ascent was made. The carousal ran 24/7 to collect money and pay the expenses of the dead aeronaut. Burke, the surviving partner said he was not frightened by Nelson's fate. He said "I expect that the same thing that happened to "Red" will some day happen to me." He may have just made a date with "Karma."

Directions:
Pioneer & Military Memorial Park
14th Avenue and Jefferson Street
Phoenix, AZ 85007
602-534-1262
www.azhistcemeteries.org

Minnie Powers: The Faded Rose

Re-enactor Cindy Lee talks about the murder of Madam Minnie Powers

Tucked away in a back corner of the Pioneer and Military Memorial Park Cemeteries is the grand madam of early Phoenix. Her name was Rose R Gregory, but she was better known as Minnie Powers to the gentlemen of Phoenix, Arizona. Rose was English and born in 1850. She had settled in Utah with her husband and daughter Mary. After her husband died, she sent three year old Mary to live with her family in the San Francisco, California area to get her a proper education. She arrived in Arizona Territory about 1878. Rose Gregory lived in Phoenix during its earliest pioneer days.

Rose became Minnie Powers and was the Madam of a house of ill repute near East Jackson Street in Phoenix. She had many friends and was loved by all because of her many acts of kindness. She was always ready to donate to the needy, help with disasters, and she saved many misfortunate people from starvation. Minnie tried to keep a low profile and rarely gave officers occasion to interfere with her bawdy house.

But, like many women who lived the sporting life, Minnie faced a sorrowful ending. She owned a saloon on East Jackson

Street in the area referred as the Reservation. It was called the Villa Road House and was located at 720 Railroad Avenue.

William Belcher, known as the "Cockney" was the bartender at the house and they had been living with each other on and off for a couple of years. Cockney was a heavy drinker and their relationship had not been running smoothly at the time. He was spending more and more time in jail than on the streets of Phoenix. And while he was locked up, other gentlemen stayed with Minnie at the house.

On September 7, 1898, he was released from the city jail yet again. After downing a few drinks, he found a revolver and headed down to Minnie Powers' house. He entered the house from the rear and proceeded straight to Minnie's room.

A few people in the area heard some shooting about 10:00 in the morning. Since nobody saw a disturbance, little attention was paid to the gunfire. At 1:00, one of her "girls"—Flora—came by the house to rent a room. She banged on the door, but could get no answer. Puzzled, she came inside and began to look for Minnie.

Minnie was found lying in her bed with her hand under her head, as though she was sleeping—which she probably was when the fatal shots were fired. They say by the peaceful expression on her face, it was evident Minnie never knew what happened. A bullet hole was visible on the right side of the head above the ear and another penetrated the center of the body a little to the right of the heart. The side of her face and the pillow was blackened by gun powder. Minnie's corpse was literally swimming in blood and it seemed the mattress could no longer absorb the crimson flow.

The lifeless corpse of Belcher lay across her ankles—with his own feet on the floor, and his right hand grasping a 44 caliber revolver. He must have stood opposite of her right side by the bed when he fired the shot into her head, then fired the second shot into her body. He then walked around to the foot of the bed. He placed the weapon into his mouth holding it with his left hand as he pulled the trigger with his right hand.

Minnie Powers' funeral was handled by undertaker Davis and they provided her with a beautiful casket. It was copper lined with silver plated handles. It had a little silver plate on the lid with the words "At Rest" inscribed. Large crowds came to view her remains each day so all her good deeds and generosity to the poor were not in vain. Dozens of flowers and roses covered her coffin as she was laid to rest.

Grave marker for Rose Gregory AKA Minnie Powers

Directions:
Pioneer & Military Memorial Park
1317 West Jefferson Street
Phoenix, AZ 85007
www.azhistcemeteries.org

The Camelback Cemetery Love Story

Hans and Mary Weaver owned a 160 acre ranch a mile or so from the Phoenix landmark, Camelback Mountain. Their lovely daughter, Hattie, fell in love and married a handsome young poultry farmer, Adolph Frank Poenicke, in 1915.

The families made big plans for the newlywed's future, but all that came to a halt just three weeks after the marriage ceremony. On May 20, 1915, Adolph suffered a hemorrhage and died leaving his beautiful bride, Hattie, a grieving widow.

Hattie was devastated. There was no nearby cemetery to bury young Poenicke. Mr. Weaver buried him on a portion of their land so Hattie could sit near his grave site often. The following year, Hans Weaver dedicated a plat of his land as Camelback Cemetery, thus making Adolph's final resting place one of Phoenix's first pioneer cemeteries.

Two years later, Han's lovely wife Mary contacted the contagious influenza, died and was buried in the cemetery near her son in law. They share the same tombstone marker.

Grave site of Mary Weaver and Adolf Poenicke

Slowly the tiny cemetery began to flourish. It is shared by the rich and poor citizens of Phoenix alike. One section of the graveyard is lined in neat little rows of white crosses. It is said these are the final resting spots for many workers of the old ranches, servants of the fine houses near Camelback Mountain, and victims of the flu epidemic. They were all buried here because they were loved. Here, the poor are honored as well as the rich and famous names resting next to them.

Grave markers of
Laura Dunn Stanley and
her son Riley

Take time to visit this treasure on along Mc Donald Drive some weekend. Along with migrant workers, you will find farmers who chose the majestic view of Camelback Mountain as their final resting place. There are folks who died from TB, children who drowned in the near by canals, along with tragic shootings, car accidents, and railroad fatalities. But the one thing they all have in common is they are all part of someone's love story and their spirits fill the tiny cemetery with their continuous devotion.

Camelback Cemetery is tucked away in a quiet Phoenix neighborhood

Directions:

Camelback Cemetery is located on the north side of the road between Mocking Bird and Scottsdale Road in Paradise Valley, AZ.

Who's In Hunts Tomb?

I remember moving to Arizona and visiting Papago Park for the first time. I was curious to know why a pyramid was towering high above a hill over looking the landscape. The locals would tease me and ask, "Do you know who's buried in Hunt's Tomb?" I would naively ask, "Who?" and they would retort, "Hunt, of course!"

My inquisitive mind became so overwhelmed that I had my former boyfriend drive me up to the monument so I could see for myself. That is when I learned that Arizona's former governor George E. P. Hunt (seven terms in office) is buried there. Also entombed are his beloved wife, in-laws, daughter, and a son in law. I was mesmerized by the beautiful view he selected as their final resting place.

George E. P. Hunt was born November 1, 1859. He was sworn in as Arizona's first governor on February 14, 1912 followed by six additional terms ending in 1932. A portly gentleman, he often referred to himself as the "Old Walrus." He was a supporter of

Arizona Governor George E P Hunt
1859-1934

reformed government and was either revered or feared by his followers. Hunt passed away December 24, 1934 and was laid to rest beside his wife in the Hunt Mausoleum.

So many ask why Governor Hunt selected a pyramid as his burial monument. A pyramid represents the primordial mound from which Egyptians believed the planet Earth was created. The shape of the pyramid represents the descending rays of the sun. The upper chambers were intended as a magical device to attract the Sun God Re on his journey across the sky. The daily encounter with Re would allow the dead to assume the role of the great Sun God in the afterlife. Others say the Pyramid was designed as a resurrection machine pointing to the stars in the Heavens.

Hunt's Tomb

The archaeology discovery of the King Tut tomb in 1922 spawned a world wide fascination for anything Egyptian. The Egypt craze or Art Deco, was popular in jewelry, fashion and building architecture. George Hunt and his family journeyed to Egypt in 1930 to visit the great pyramids and monuments. The trip sparked his desire to search for a location to build his own pyramid and be buried in a mausoleum for all eternity.

Hunt was granted permission from Congress to build his 30 foot by 20 foot pyramid on a small piece of the 2,050 acres that had been set aside as Papago Saguaro National Monument. The portion of land now belongs to the City of Phoenix and in Papago Park. It is built of a concrete foundation and covered with 4 inch white polished tiles. The pyramid can be seen from almost anywhere in the park.

As the construction of the mausoleum was being constructed, Hunted was quoted to say, "The people of this state have been good to me and in my last sleep I want to be buried so that I may in my spirit look over this splendid valley that in years to come will be a Mecca of those that love beautiful things and in the state where people rule."

I have a feeling his ghost is keeping a close eye on events down at the State Capital today!

Directions:

The Hunt Tomb is on the west side of Papago Park, overlooking the Phoenix Zoo and the park. Take the turn for the entrance to the Phoenix Zoo at 455 N. Galvin Parkway, but turn to the left to the picnic area instead of entering the zoo parking lot. Turn left again at a second entrance to the zoo parking lot. (It will appear that the first two turns take you away from the Tomb which is visible from most of the road.) At the next intersection, turn right following the sign to Hunt's Tomb. Stay on that road, bearing right as it winds up the hill to the parking lot. The Tomb is a few steps to the east of the parking lot.

Double Buttes Cemetery Ghostly Pioneers

Double Buttes Cemetery was established in 1897. Many Tempe residents and who played key roles in the leadership and history of the State of Arizona are interred in Double Butte Cemetery. Sections A, B, C, and D are the areas of the graveyard which the Tempe Cemetery Company first began selling family lots. It is now known as the Pioneer Section.

Some of these famous pioneers are known to haunt their former homes or establishments. Could these ghosts haunt the Double Buttes Cemetery as well? Do they use their burial plots as some kind of a terminal where they can come and go to the places scores of people have witnessed their presence?

Gravestone for Carl Hayden

Monti's La Casa Vieja is the original adobe hacienda built by Charles Trumbull Hayden in 1871. Hayden settled in the area to start a flour mill and ferry service for crossing the Salt River which flowed year round back then. You might see an image of a cowboy resembling Hayden vanish before your eyes in the Mural Room. The sound of children's laughter is often heard in the Fountain Room. Hayden's grave lies in the Hayden family plot near the front entrance of Double Buttes Cemetery. His son, Senator Carl Hayden grew up at Hayden's Ferry. He rests in a plot nearby.

Grave marker for Eliza Teeter

Farther east we find the grave of Eliza Teeter. She was widowed at a young age and ran a Phoenix boarding house to make ends meet. She died in the back bedroom of the home which is now called the Garden Dining Room at the Teeter House Tea Room. Her ghost has been seen walking through the restaurant. Kitchen items have moved to other areas or turned up missing. Teeter's ghost has been suspected of hiding keys under the kitchen sink. She rests peacefully beside the tombstone of her beloved husband.

Casey Moore's Oyster House has been a trendy bar scene in Tempe for several years, but it was once the residence of William and Mary Mouer—part of the prominent Mouer family along Ash Street. The couple both died separate —one in front of the downstairs fireplace and the other in the upstairs bedroom. Reports of dancing ghostly silhouettes, thought to be the Mouer's, have been witnessed by neighbors from time to time. The couple lies side by side in the Mouer Family plot for an eternal waltz.

As you begin to investigate the ghosts of the Hayden's at Monti's La Casa Vieja, Mrs. Teeter at the Teeter House Team Room, and the Mouer's at Casey Moore's Oyster House, be sure to include a stop at the very haunted Double Butte's Cemetery and see if they have come home for the night.

Directions:

Monti's La Casa Vieja
100 S Mill Avenue
Tempe, AZ 85281
480-967-7594
www.montis.com

Teeter House Tea Room
622 E Adams Street
Phoenix, AZ 85004
602-252-4682
www.theteeterhouse.com

Casey Moore's Oyster House
850 S Ash Avenue
Tempe, AZ 85281
480-968-9935
www.caseymoores.com
Double Buttes Cemetery
2505 W Broadway Road
Tempe, AZ 85282

Henry Wickenburg's Grave Site

Henry Wickenburg
1819-1905

Henry Wickenburg was born in November 1819 and was a native of Austria. He sailed to the United States in 1847 and settled briefly in New York. Before long, the excitement of the Gold Rush in the West drew him out to the San Francisco area where he learned to pan for gold. His travels brought him to the Arizona Territory in 1862 near Fort Yuma.

Wickenburg eventually traveled along the La Paz River and ended up near the Hassayampa River with several other prospectors in hopes of locating a gold mine. Leaving the other men behind, Henry Wickenburg traveled back to an area of big white cropping near Vulture City. It was there he discovered the Vulture Mine in 1863. Vulture City is about fifteen miles from the town of Wickenburg.

He later settled in the town that bears his name and tried his hand at ranching and farming. Flood waters destroyed his crops and livestock which unfortunately brought his ranching dream to an end. The lifelong bachelor resided at his small adobe ranch house near the Hassayampa until he died in May 1905. Wickenburg did not possess much property or valuables at the time of his death. He took his own life by putting a bullet to his head. His obituary states he was "quite melancholy due to old age, weakening mental vigor, and the lack of family ties that bind one more strongly than anything to this world."

During Cemetery Crawl 5 the teams were instructed to photograph the grave site of Henry Wickenburg. The teams were having a difficult time locating the small cemetery hidden in a residential neighborhood. The Ghostie Geckos team was hot on the trail. Driving near the site, Cindy Lee noticed an elderly man in a dark suit pointing to something across the road on a hill. The team pulled over and when they looked back, the man was gone. They looked in the direction where he was pointing and saw the flagpole that marks the cemetery where Wickenburg is buried. Later, Cindy was looking through some historical photos and identified the man she saw to be Henry Wickenburg.

Gravesite of Henry Wickenburg

Directions:

The town of Wickenburg now surrounds his gravesite that sits on the top of a hill in a local neighborhood. It is a bit tricky to locate the first time—or even the second time—but well worth the search. From Highway 60, turn left on S Jefferson Street. Jefferson winds on to Fisher Street. Make a left turn on to Adams. Adams then turns into Howard Court. Immediately begin looking to your left for a flag pole on the top of a hill. Park your car and take the walking path to the summit and you will find the grave of Henry Wickenburg and a few other Wickenburg pioneers.

Ghostly Farmer at the Wittmann Cemetery

The tiny cemetery of Wittmann is tucked away east of Highway 60 about half way from between Phoenix and Wickenburg. The community was named for one of the investors who financed the plans to reconstruct the Walnut Grove Dam. The Walnut Grove Dam at the Hassayampa River collapsed on February 22, 1890. Between 50 and 150 people died in the flood. Up until then, Wittmann was called Nadaburg. The town folk were so grateful of Wittmann's interest in dam and the irrigation needs of the area, that they changed the name of the town to Wittmann in the 1930's.

Entrance to the Whitman Cemetery

Wittmann Cemetery is one of the first cemeteries I ever investigated. For years the rumor of a ghost of an old farmer has been circulating. They say the farmer wearing a hat and overalls is seen walking near the cemetery gate late at night and floating towards the Iona Wash. One evening I decided to drive up to Wittmann and meet another investigating team taking photos in the Wittmann Cemetery. I brought along my daughter Nikki and we drove up Highway 60 towards Wickenburg. I had vague directions, but I was certain I would find the graveyard. I always do.

It was pitched black when I turned off 211th Avenue and followed the sign directing us to the cemetery. The only way I was able to find my fellow ghost hunters was by the flash of their digital cameras. We spent a couple of hours walking around snapping photos and gathering the usual collections of dust orbs on film. But in those early days, that was really something!

The gravesite of Copper Penny

Recently, we made the Wittmann Cemetery one of the stops on Cemetery Crawl 4—a road rally that travels around Arizona to study various cemetery styles and sizes. I was amazed how the housing developments are slowing closing in around the small cemetery which is still in use. Most graves range from the 1940's to the present. The most interesting tombstone is one of Copper Penny who passed away on 6 AUG 1987. The grave is adorned with several coins and pennies. Wittmann Cemetery is maintained by the Saguaro Janes Group of volunteers. Some headstones are stamped unknown. The entrance gate is along Galvin Road which is the East side of the cemetery.

We never did see the ghost of the old farmer during our visits—but you just never know what ghosts you might reap on a lonely road in the countryside.

Directions:

Wittmann Cemetery is East of Hwy 60 about half way (25 miles) between Wickenburg and Phoenix. Approaching Wittmann, look to your right for Center Street. Turn Right. Near the school, turn right on West Dove Valley Road. Turn left at 211th Avenue. Drive about 1 mile. Watch for a cemetery sign. Turn left on West Galvin Street. Drive down road. Cemetery will be on your left. Park outside Cemetery Gate

Mohave County

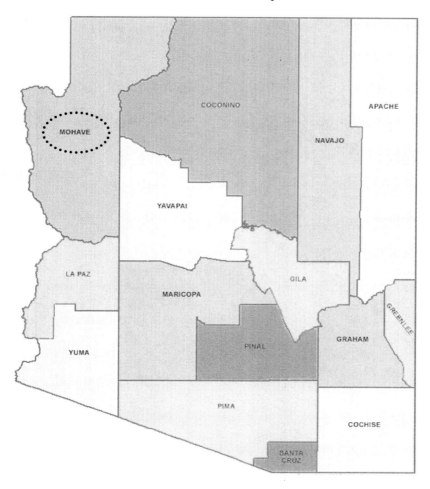

Ghosts at the Goal Posts

The football stadium at White Cliff Middle School in Kingman, AZ gives an entirely different meaning to the term "team spirit". This football field was built on what was once the Pioneer Cemetery of Kingman. The Pioneer Cemetery was known as the original cemetery in Kingman from 1900 to 1917.

Until recently this was believed to be Jennie Bauters

About 1903, Jennie Bauters—Jerome's most famous and loved madam—left Jerome, AZ and headed for a new boom town called Acne (now known as Goldfield). Jennie's gambling suitor, Clement C. Leigh, followed her there. After a time, Jennie began to feel he was becoming somewhat of a threat. In September 1905, Leigh needed money to settle a bad debt. With anger and a gun in his hand, he bounded over to Jennie's place and demanded she hand over all her cash. An argument ensued and Jennie tried to flee the building. He chased after her, firing several shots at the frightened woman. On bullet struck and wounded her as she ran frantically out into the street. He approached the paralyzed woman and fired a fatal shot to her head. He then pointed the gun to his chest and fired again. He lay down beside Jennie—ready to die. Instead, Leigh survived his suicide attempt and was carted off to jail. Jennie was mourned by all who loved her, and laid to rest in the Pioneer Cemetery in Kingman. In 1907, justice was served and Leigh was hung. He too, was buried in the Kingman Pioneer Cemetery.

In 1917, the county began the task of moving the graves of the dearly departed to the new Mountain View Cemetery. Mohave County did not pay for your loved ones to be moved to the new location. That was the family's responsibility. So, some of the not so dearly departed, whose relatives would not come forward, were not moved. They were left behind at the deserted cemetery.

Jenny Bauters is seen dressed in black on the balcony of this brothel

Mohave County donated the old Pioneer Cemetery property to the school board to build a new high school. A stadium and parking lot replaced the hallowed grounds. They say that in the 1940's, a group of youngsters playing on the football field began to unearth bones of the bodies that were never moved to Mountain View Cemetery. Many local organizations were alarmed. They immediately took action and had the existing remains exhumed and placed in a solitary grave on the property. There is a plaque dedicated to the unknown buried pioneers on the school grounds. The old high school is now a Kingman middle school.

And, as fate would have it, Jennie Bauters and her murderer, Clement Leigh, are now buried in the same grave and entombed forever in the end zone of a football field. So if you are ever attending a big football game at the old stadium and the excitement begins to magnify—beware the *rising spirits* might be more than just the cheering crowd.

Directions:
The Pioneer Cemetery was located at the present site of the Bill Williams High School Stadium and parking lot.

Pinal County

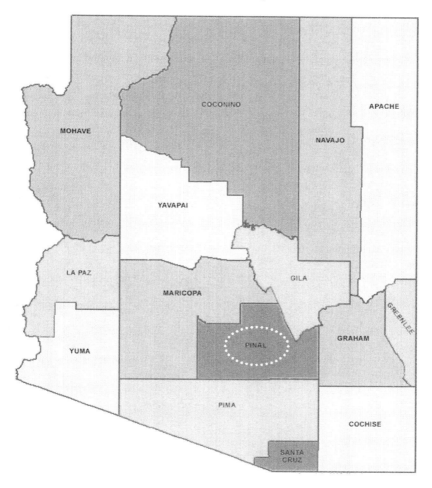

The Lost City of Adamsville

From the lost city of the Hohokam in Casa Grande, the MVD Ghostchasers workshop crew caravanned to yet a more modern day lost town site—Adamsville—and the lost City of Adamsville Cemetery. Adamsville was founded by Charles Adams in the 1870's. At its peak, Adamsville had 400 inhabitants, stores, a flour mill, and water tanks. The town site was eventually deserted and the flooding waters of the Gila River washed away of what remained of Adamsville. The Cemetery lingers with tombstones scattered across the graveyard dating back to 1877.

Once the group arrived, we showed our good intentions of visiting the cemetery by donning gloves and packing several trash bags with broken glass, bottles, and garbage other visitors had left behind. There are rumors of satanic rituals performed at the site so we did our best to add positive energy around us.

Tombstone of Mary A Carpenter

At dusk, we began to fill the next several hours photographing the tombstones in this mysterious cemetery. We practiced grave dowsing using our divining rods. Some tried their hand at recording EVP, while others say they received messages from beyond.

Several Masons have their grave markers erected directly on the 33rd parallel which we found very interesting. The 33rd parallel north latitude runs through Arizona, nearer to absolute 33rd parallel in towns like Florence and Clifton. Neighboring places like Chandler, Ahwatukee and Maricopa all share the 33rd parallel. The Adamsville Cemetery is located on it and a medicine wheel in stone is placed in the center of the consecrated grounds. It appears from the way the graves are laid out, that the Masons buried in the cemetery were lining up along the parallel. The 33rd parallel has been associated with Freemasonry as symbolic latitude. Although there has always been a great deal of secrecy concerning its importance, the 33rd parallel been associated with places of extreme conflict and death.

Energy Circle at Adamsville Cemeter

A medicine wheel is usually located where the Earth's energy is very strong. Because of the vortex energy, these places are of intense power and healing. Many visit the wheels to seek visions or communicate with the dead. We took turns standing in the center of the wheel to experience the healing powers. As you stand in the medicine wheel, face north and hold out your arms. You will feel the energy of the 33rd parallel run through both arms. We took a unique group photo standing in the center of the medicine wheel.

We all agreed due to the location—the 33rd parallel—this cemetery was very active. Hopefully the site will be historically preserved and maintained for future visitors.

Sunset over Adamsville Cemetery

Directions:

On the south edge of the town of Florence is the junction of Highway 79 and 287. 3.5 miles from the junction, you will find a historical marker telling about Adamsville. Just past the marker, turn north on Adamsville Road and follow it for 2.8 miles. Just after the road curves to the right, watch for a driveway turning off to the left. It is difficult to see the A.O.U.W. cemetery from the road.

Above: The author stands in the center of the energy circle

Middle: An open book graces the top of a tombstone

Below: Cemetery grounds at Adamsville Cemetery

Charles D. Poston and His Temple to the Sun

Charles D Poston
1825-1902

Colonel Charles D. Poston was what one would call a visionary or a dreamer. He is better known as the Father of Arizona. Born in Kentucky on April 29, 1825, Poston was appointed by President Lincoln as the superintendent of Indian affairs in 1863. He was the first delegate to the US Congress from the Arizona Territory in 1863.

Poston traveled to India and became familiar with Parsee religion. He became a Zoroastrian soon after his return to the United States. Zoroastrians consider fire as a medium to which spiritual insight and wisdom is gained. He built a pyramid shaped fire temple near Florence and envisioned the spot to be where Indians once worshiped a sun God. He called his fire temple the "Parsee Hill"—a place he could go to pray and gain knowledge. After a few months, the flames died out. People mocked the temple calling it "Poston's Folly".

Charles Poston became feeble in his later years and his health declined rapidly. Suffering from occasional fainting spells, he refused to give up his independence and preferred to be alone. Poston took a tumble in the alley leading to the back of his home and was found unconscious by a local Phoenix police officer. The former president of the early Arizona Historical society died of natural causes. He was nearly broke and had no relatives to fulfill his wish to be buried on his "sacred mountain". Instead he was interred in a simple grave in Porter Cemetery, one of the seven cemeteries that make up the Pioneer & Military Memorial Park in Phoenix.

Twenty-three years after his death, the metal casket containing Poston's remains were removed from the old Phoenix cemetery. They were transported just west of Florence, Arizona and north of the Gila River to celebrate the 100th anniversary of his birth. He was reburied on Parsee Hill (Primrose Hill) which was renamed Poston Butte—the very place where he was never able to complete his "Temple to the Sun". He was entombed in a pyramid structure in an official ceremony led by Governor George W P Hunt, whom by the way, was later entombed in his *own* pyramid high on a hill in Papago Park in Phoenix.

Poston's Tomb at Poston Butte

Directions:
Turn west on Hunt Highway just two miles north of Florence, AZ. Drive about 1.5 miles and watch for Poston Butte sign and turn north on dirt road. Drive under the RR tracks and follow dirt road east of the Butte. Park and walk up the .5 mile walkway.

The Hunt for Mattie Earp

Mattie Earp
1850-1888

As you have read in previous stories, my paranormal team enjoys road trips to find grave sites of members of the Earp saga. One of the first grave sites we tried to locate was Mattie Blaylock Earp—Wyatt's common law wife. Mattie resided with Earp in Tombstone during their short stay in "the town too tough to die".

Mattie traveled west with the Earp family when they took Morgan Earp's body for burial in California. She later returned to Arizona searching for Wyatt. He had already left the Arizona Territory with the love of his life, Josephine. Mattie met up with Big Nose Kate in Globe, AZ where they worked the bawdy houses together. She then headed to the boom town of Pinal, AZ during its glory days. Depressed over the loss of Wyatt and her unfortunate lifestyle, Mattie died of an overdose of whiskey and laudanum on July 3, 1888 in Pinal, Arizona. She was only 38 years old.

Our first attempt to locate the old Pinal Cemetery where Mattie is buried failed. With only a hand drawn map and vague directions, we drove up and down the back roads off US Hwy 60 at least a dozen times. We never saw any of the landmarks described on the map. We called the search off and headed home. The second try was cut even shorter. US 60 was closed because of a serious vehicle collision, and we were rerouted straight back to Phoenix.

We finally had success on our third excursion. Nancy, Shiela and I vowed this would be the day we would find Mattie Earp's grave. We drove 60 miles east to Superior, turned on Silver King Road and headed in the direction described on our hand written map. If we didn't find it on our first try, we would drive into town and find an old timer that would surely know where Pinal Cemetery was. And of course, we did not find the cemetery the first time. Heading back towards the main highway, we spied a mobile home off to the right side of the road.

We pulled in their driveway and parked Shiela's truck. Nancy climbed out of the passenger seat and knocked on the front door of the mobile home. A gentleman holding a can of beer opened the screen door to greet Nancy. She politely asked for directions to Mattie Earp's grave.

The man and his buddies were busy watching football. He promised they would lead the way to the cemetery as soon as it was half time. You see, it was Super Bowl Sunday and they were not about to miss a play. About ten minutes later, three men emerged from the house and piled into their own pickup truck. They motioned for us to follow them and soon we were heading in the same area on the back roads where we had just came from.

Fortunately, these men knew the correct turnoff to the desert roadway that led to the cemetery. We drove past the white bee keeper houses, past the discarded swamp cooler and box frame mattress. We drove gingerly through the field of glass and the rutted dirt road. Bushes and Palo Verde trees gave the truck a new set of "desert pin striping."

"Great", Nancy sighed, "Here is another fine fix you've got us in. We are following a bunch of strange drunk men we don't know into the desert. This is scary!"

"Don't worry," I said from the backseat, "I have the camcorder on and I am filming their license plate number in case something happens."

"Ya," laughed Shiela, "Just hope the sheriff finds our bodies *and* the camcorder."

Flowers adorn the memorial to Mattie Earp

Finally, just off to the right we saw what we came to see! The railroad tie marker erected in the memory of the forgotten woman, Mattie Earp. We leapt out of the truck and began snapping pictures. The men stood by their truck with arms folded. They seemed amused.

"So you ladies came all the way out here just to see this?" they chuckled.

"We're ghost hunters," I told them.

Their faces went blank. Who was scared now? They looked at each other and quickly hopped back into their pick up truck. Maybe we made *them* at tad nervous—or maybe the half time show was about over. I never seen grown men move so fast!

We spent the next hour exploring the tiny cemetery, picking up garbage, and taking photos of the tombstones. We ended our visit by leaving an airline size bottle of whiskey for Mattie on top of her grave marker.

Since that day, we have conducted many Spirit Photo Workshops at the Pinal Cemetery. Several of us return time and again to spend the evening with Mattie to do EVP sessions and photograph the area. There are reports of a separate tombstone marker that may be Mattie's actual resting place, but cemetery dowsers feel the railroad tie marker is the real thing. Take a drive to Superior, bring Mattie some wild flowers, and be sure to toast her short, but interesting life.

Another view of the Mattie Earp memorial marker in Pinal Cemetery

---

Directions:

Travel East from Phoenix on US Highway 60. As you approached Superior, AZ turn left on Silver King Road. Bear left onto Happy Camp Road. After you go up hill, turn left into the desert. Immediately bear right. Stay on rutted road about .6 miles. The Cemetery will be on your right.

Pima County

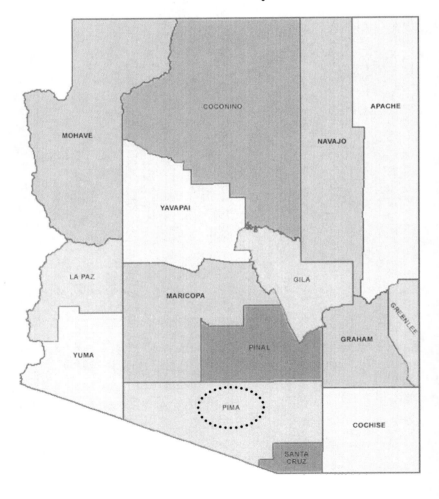

The Hunt For Johnny Behan

Johnny H Beham
1845-1912

We began our search for John Behan in April of 2008 as we scouted cemeteries for the famed Arizona road rally called Cemetery Crawl 3. Our theme for this run was "Bad men and Lawmen." I had learned former Sheriff John Behan was buried—or had a commemorated marker in Holy Hope Cemetery in Tucson, so the hunt was on!

John Harris Behan was born in Missouri on October 23, 1845. He served a two-year term as the sheriff of Cochise County in the growing Arizona Territory from February 1881 to November 1882. This newly created county included the famous mining boon town of Tombstone. Behan is known for being the county sheriff during the controversial gunfight at the OK Corral and later involved in the Earp vendetta ride for justice.

Behan later became a deputy warden at the Yuma Territorial Prison in Yuma, AZ. He also served as a quarter master soldier in the Spanish American War. His successful career in law enforcement ended in 1912. John Behan died at St Mary's Catholic Hospital on June 7, 1912 in Tucson. He was buried as a Catholic in Tucson's Holy Hope Cemetery one day after his death on June 8, 1912.

Shiela and I pulled into the Holy Hope Cemetery gates and headed for the older section of the cemetery. It was quite overwhelming when we noted the size of the cemetery which butts against its counterpart—Evergreen Cemetery. After a drive through the ornate grounds we decided a trip to the cemetery office would definitely aid our search. We walked into the building and waited while a clerk finished her phone call.

Johnny Beham rests in Holy Hope Cemetery in Tucson

"Could you please give us directions to the grave of Johnny Behan," I asked.

She didn't say a word but quickly grabbed a map of the cemetery and began to draw arrows and marked the lot and space number on the grid.

"Apparently, I am not the first person to ask that question," I winked at Shiela.

Soon we were back in the car and heading back in the direction we had just come. We were not far off from our original search, but thankful we now had the map where "X" marks the spot. We each took a row of graves and started our way down the green, grassy pathway.

"Found it!" I shouted with pride.

And there he was…lying with many other citizens of Tucson who were pioneers in making Arizona one of the most historic states in the West. Another resting place of a member of the Earp saga had been found. We placed a red rose on the grave and offered a moment of silence.

Grave site of Johnny Beham

Directions:
Holy Hope Cemetery
3555 N Oracle Road
Tucson, AZ 85705
Go to Block B
Row G (9)
Grave 98

Yavapai County

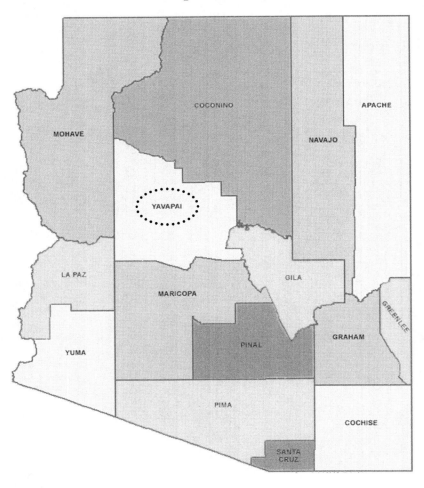

Ghostly Mists of Clear Creek Cemetery

Entrance to Clear Creek Cemetery

Camp Verde, Arizona boasts the historic Clear Creek Church and Clear Creek Cemetery as a great way to discover and learn about the history of Verde Valley. The cemetery covers five acres of land that was once site of the earliest settlements in the valley. The charming little cemetery is the final resting spot to some of these early pioneers—it is also known to have a few lively spirits.

The early settlement, where Clear Creek meets with the Verde River, consisted of farming families. The easy access to water and the rich soil provided the small community with fine crops. Clear Creek is near the site of the first Forte Verde—or Fort Lincoln, as it was named—and was occupied by soldiers from Prescott. These men came to protect the settlers from the Yavapai and Apache Indians who had earlier claims to the rich farmland.

Clear Creek Church and Cemetery are just a few miles away from the present city center of Camp Verde. The site of the fort had also moved up to the other bank of the river over the years. The cemetery still remains a big part of Camp Verde history and is still in use today. With new housing developments popping up all around the cemetery, it is barely out in the countryside these days.

The earliest burial found and recorded is dated 1868. A despondent 17 year old girl in the settlement committed suicide and was laid to rest in what is now the oldest section of the cemetery. Maggie Farrell's grave is marked only by a metal name plate. No monument honors her short life.

One can hardly miss the Wingfield family plot. A botched robbery at the old Wingfield mercantile claimed the lives of Robert Mac Rodgers and Clinton Wingfield. Rodgers' was shot by the assailant near the doorway of the store. Clinton Wingfield, heard the gunshots, came out of a back room and was also shot. The bullet entered his chest and lodged in his spine, paralyzing him instantly. They carried him back across the street to the main room of the stage stop building and gave him medical treatment. He died two hours later in front of the fireplace. Wingfield and Rodger's graves stand side by side in the cement bordered plot.

Tombstones of Clinton Wingfield and Robert Mac Rodgers

Cemetery Crawl 5 recently paid a visit to the Clear Creek Cemetery. Teams traveled to remote areas of Arizona on a road rally that offered a look at various size and types of cemeteries. Deb and Judy of the Verde Valley Spirit Seekers were one hand to host the Clear Creek Cemetery and told a few tales of their paranormal investigations in the old graveyard.

Debbie said she has a couple pictures with a mysterious mist from the cemetery. One photo was taken of a grave that was partially dug out. She believed they were re-decorating it, because it didn't look like vandalism. It was a double grave, with mist rising from the husband's side.

One other evening, her nephew was carrying the cell sensor, and the alarm started going off. Deb snapped a picture of him, and he had a strange mist around him, too. Her son James picked up an EVP that sounded like a group of children shrieking or laughing in the distance and there was nobody else around. Across the road is the Old Clear Creek Church...can some of these restless spirits be seeking redemption into the world beyond?

Clear Creek Church

Directions:
From Phoenix: Head north on the I 17 to Camp Verde exit 285. Follow General Crook Trail to the HWY 60-89 East. Turn on Old Church Road and follow to cemetery.

Misty Ghosts of Congress

The ghost town of Congress is located just a little north of Wickenburg, Arizona. Its post office was established in January 1889 and discontinued in August 1928. Gold was discovered by Dennis May in 1884 and more than 400 men came to work in the mines. There were two sections of Congress, "Mill town" and "Lower town", the later of which featured the homes and general businesses. Congress even boasted its own electric light plant. But, like most towns in the desert, water was scarce. A fire in 1898 destroyed many of the businesses in Congress. The mines tapped out in the 1930's, and the town lived on as a railroad station known today as Congress Junction.

Entrance to the old Congress Cemetery

There are remnants of a few old structures including an old mine and a couple of old cemeteries known to be haunted. The Congress Pioneer Cemetery lays near the hills of the old mine. There are at least 100 graves, mostly unmarked. Eight of the grave sites are enclosed by decorative wrought iron enclosures, and a few others are surrounded by old weathered wooden fences. Some graves are covered with stone or completely blanketed by cacti.

The burials in the old Pioneer Cemetery took place between 1887 and 1954. The newer cemetery has been in use since 1910. The old Congress Pioneer Cemetery was featured as a stop along the route of Cemetery Crawl 2—the popular road rally established by the MVD Ghostchasers as a way to view various types of cemeteries in Arizona. This cemetery has been a favorite with ghost hunters for recording EVP (Electronic Voice Phenomena) and for photographing amoralities of spirits amongst the tombstones.

Tombstones of Joseph Giacomino (left) and Matilde B Brady (right)

Mark, Kenton and I were assigned to the third cemetery stop on the route which just happened to be the old Congress Pioneer Cemetery. As we waited for the "Cemetery Crawlers" to arrive, it began to rain. I stood in the roadway watching for the eight teams to get there while the men looked on from the pickup truck. I suddenly noticed something odd about a half mile down the road in the newer (but old) Congress Cemetery. I saw two people walking about the cemetery as if they were looking for a loved one. Dressed in light clothing, I thought they might be members of the Cemetery Crawl who had stopped at the wrong cemetery and were trying to find the grave marker on their poetic clue sheet.

Darkness falls in Congress Cemetery

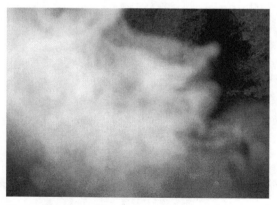

Eerie mists are often seen on the cemetery grounds

Mark and Kenton saw the same figures I did. I sent them down the road to direct the lost team to back to the cemetery where we had been waiting. I grabbed the umbrella and kept my vigil at the Pioneer Cemetery entrance. About ten minutes later, Mark and Kenton returned with a puzzled look on their faces.

"Did you send the team over here?" I asked scanning my check in sheet.

"There was nobody up there," Kenton scratch his head. "There was no vehicle—no people—no footprints on the wet ground."

"But, all three of us saw "someone" walking in the cemetery," confirmed Mark.

"Well, boys," I grinned from ear to ear, "I think we just saw ourselves a couple of ghosts!"

Directions:
From Phoenix, take I-17 (the Black Canyon Freeway) to US 60 West to Wickenburg. Take US 93 to State Route 89 towards Congress Jct. Go ½ mile on State Rte 71—then turn on Ghost Town Road. Watch for signs that will direct you to the cemeteries.

Ghostly Surprise in the Jerome Cemetery

Once known as the "Wickedest town in the West", Jerome was a copper mining camp, evolving from a few tents and shacks to a roaring mining community of mansions and quaint Victorian homes. Jerome was once the fourth largest city in the Arizona Territory. The population peaked at 15,000 during the 1920's. The mines abruptly closed in 1953. The residents packed up their belongings and left town, turning Jerome into a "Ghost City." Today the town is home to about 450 souls who promote the hillside community as a historic ghost town.

Rod iron gates still grace the cemetery

Men and women from all over the world flocked to Arizona to find work, wealth, and a successful life in the West. They brought their families and did whatever it took to feed and clothe them.

Some of these pioneers met with tragedies such as disease, murder, suicide, and mining accidents. A cemetery was established on a near by hill that overlooked the town of Jerome, and had spectacular views of the Verde Valley.

Some of these pioneers died too soon, and some Jerome residents say ghosts wander about the cemetery seeking redemption, while others are doomed to be lost in a world they could not tame. Visitors to the old cemetery have seen shadowy dark figures moving between the tombstones dated form 1897 to 1942. Sometimes footsteps are heard as if someone is following close behind you. Paranormal investigators doing EVP work have heard and recorded voices on the north end of the graveyard.

The MVD Ghostchasers paranormal team and guests have explored this turn of the century burial ground on several occasions. Just driving to the cemetery gate can be spellbinding in itself. As you exit Jerome on Highway 89, you must make a sharp left turn on a tiny road called North Street that immediately drops downward at a slanted angle. The dirt road ends at the cemetery gate. You must exit your vehicle to walk the worn paths among the old crosses and tombstones.

Tombstones lean in the old Jerome Cemetery

One evening the group was quietly snapping photographs in the dark when a small group of the ghost hunters heard what sounded like footsteps just to the northwest end of the cemetery. They stood still in silence in order to focus on which direction they should start walking to find their ghost. Soon a ghostly moan

Sunset over the tombstone of Clara Lanzendorf

filtered through the air. The group huddled together for they had no clue what they were about to encounter at the top of the knoll. Slowly they crept up the side of the hill. Just as they reached the top, the pitiful moaned filled the night air once again. They quickly whipped their flashlights in the direction where the dreadful moan bellowed in the moonlight. One of the ladies gasped out loud. The beam of the flashlight shone brightly on the ghostly culprit—a 50 pound Javalina.

Directions:
Drive east through Jerome on Highway 89A. Look for a street named "North Avenue". It abruptly goes north at a sharp angle and turns down a steep hill. Continue on the road until you see the cemetery.

Angeline's Grave

I first learned of Angeline's grave from a co worker. He told me that he and his friends from high school would drive out to the grave site and camp near by. They would dare each other to climb over the iron fence and stand near the grave of little Angeline. He reported the eerie tombstone glowed in the dark and the ground trembled whenever a brave soul climbed over the forbidden fence.

Grave of little Angeline Hoagland

Well, naturally I needed to go there and test the earthquake tremors out myself. But, before I made the journey to visit this misfortune little soul, I needed to learn more about Angeline. Being a member of the Pioneer's Cemetery Association in Phoenix, Arizona led to me contact one of the members of the Yavapai Cemetery

Association in Prescott, Arizona—the nearest town to the grave of Angeline.

She sent me several old newspaper articles that told the plight of this young pioneer. Angeline was born about October 1, 1886. Her short life ended on January 15, 1889 near the town of Prescott, Arizona. Her resting place sits near the bank of Lynx Creek in what is now Lynx Estates. The grave is on private property along Lynx Creek Road—also known as the Old Black Canyon Highway.

Tales of Angeline's death state she died on a wagon train heading west, and was buried on the spot. Another version of the story says she was killed by Indians, or she was attacked and killed by a Lynx cat. Others claim her family lived on Lynx Creek near their placer-mining claim. It is believed that Angeline was stricken with pneumonia. Her parents, David and Catherine Hoagland, were taking her to a doctor in Phoenix when she died along the way. Without explanation, they buried sweet Angeline at the spot where she died. What ever the case might have been, Angeline was not forgotten by her family or generations of residents of Prescott thereafter.

When the ore ran out near the tiny mining settlement near Angeline's grave, the residents moved on into Prescott and the buildings eventually eroded away. David Hoagland is rumored to have left the family unit, while Catherine stayed behind in Prescott. She took in washing and ironing and lived out her life on the corner of Sheldon and Virginia Streets.

It has been said that Angeline's grave is haunted. The tale of the tombstone glowing in the dark might have a simple explanation. It is made from a stone with minerals that absorb light during the sun lit hours, and becomes luminous after dark. When the passing cars shine their headlights on the headstone it appears to be glowing in the dark.

After receiving special instructions in how to locate Angeline's grave, the MVD Ghostchasers drove out to the site to snap a few photos and to test the glow in the dark tombstone. Chris leaped over the iron fence to pose by the grave and reported the ground did not shake or tremble. He just felt the joy this little girl must have brought to her family in her short life. We tidied up the gravesite and placed a fallen vase back on its pedestal.

Sharlot Hall, the celebrated writer and poet of the late 1800's, wrote the poem which became the inscription on Angeline's headstone.

Here lies our baby Angeline
For which we weep and do repine.
She was all our joy and all our pride
Until the day our baby died.
We hope in heaven again to meet
And then our joy will be complete.
But until our Maker calls us there
We trust her to His righteous care.

Flowers decorate Angeline's grave

Directions:

If you are in the Prescott area for the weekend, take a little side trip back in time down the old Black Canyon Highway. Look off to your left as you pass by Lynx Creek. Glowing off to the distance you will find Miss Angeline's tombstone. Don't forget to bring the flowers!

The Hunt for Big Nose Kate

Mary K Cummings
1850-1940

The simple grave site of Mary Katherine Haroney Cummings is near the bottom of the hill at the peaceful Pioneer Cemetery in Prescott, Arizona. Mary E Cummings is better known in the West as "Big Nose Kate". She was the girlfriend and common law wife of Doc Holliday of the Earp saga. Mary was born in Budapest, Hungry in 1850 to a wealthy physician. She and her siblings had good education and Mary spoke several languages. In 1862, the Emperor of Mexico contracted Dr Haroney as his personal surgeon. When the emperors' reign crumbled, her family escaped out of Mexico and moved to Davenport, IA in 1865.

After the death of her parents, Mary ran away and began to travel in the West as a dance hall girl and lived the life of a prostitute. She was an attractive, voluminous woman with a fast temper. Due to her prominent nose, she was dubbed Big Nose Kate by her customers and friends. A few years later, Kate Elder—another one of her working girl names, was employed under Bessie Earp (James Earp's wife) in Kansas. She met Doc Holliday in Ft. Griffin, Texas about 1877. They became life long companions. The bond was always intense and what you would call an "on again and off again" relationship.

After the famous gun fight in Tombstone, the Earp's packed up and moved on to California. Kate stayed in Arizona and opened a boarding house for miners in Globe. Mattie Earp worked with Kate for a short time at the Globe bawdy house. Mattie ventured on to Pinal, Arizona where she later suffered an untimely death. Doc Holliday died in Glenwood Springs, Colorado in 1887. Kate is rumored to been living in the area as well. She married a blacksmith in Colorado by the name of George Cummings in 1898. They moved back to Arizona and she ended the marriage with Cummings a couple of years later. Kate worked in Cochise, AZ running a boarding house. She was a madam in several brothels in the busy mining communities. She eventually worked as a housekeeper for a gentleman in Dos Cabezas, AZ until he died in 1930.

The aged woman petitioned to the Arizona Pioneer Home in Prescott for residency. Kate had never applied for citizenship of the United States. Although she somewhat made an impact on Arizona history, it was not in a manner historians like to mention. It is said she knew Governor George W P Hunt up in Globe before his legislation days. She wrote to the former governor seeking a recommendation to the Pioneer Home in Prescott. After a six month wait, she was finally accepted and one of the first women in Arizona to be admitted to the Pioneer Home.

Kate passed away on November 2, 1940, one week before her 90th birthday. She was laid to rest nearby at the Pioneer Cemetery in Prescott and her modest head stone reads:

Mary K Cummings
1850—1940

I was staying at Hassayampa Inn located in Prescott on a business trip. Before I left home, I had looked up the location of Kate's grave site and planned to visit and take a few pictures. After my meeting was over, I drove to the cemetery and looked for my notes. I started to panic when they couldn't be found. I knew what section of the cemetery to look in—but there were several rows and it was starting to get dark. I grabbed my cell phone and called home to speak to my daughter, Nikki. She immediately accessed the computer and directed me per phone from directions posted on FIND A GRAVE at the time. I found the tombstone within minutes and was spellbound by flowers left as tributes to this woman with the questionable past.

Grave of Mary K Cummings AKA Big Nose Kate

I thought about all the great history she witnessed—the growth of Arizona that immerged from a Wild West Territory not so long ago. Stories she told during her stay at the Pioneer Home must have mesmerized the staff and other residents. They say "if tombstones could only talk". We ghost hunters believe they do! So, I plan on going back to Prescott with a digital recording device and record whatever secrets she wishes to share on how to live a long and adventurous life!

Kate once described her life: *"Part is funny and part is sad, but such is life any way you take it."*

Directions:
From Gurley Street in Prescott, AZ head West on AZ-89/E Gurley St Toward N Virginia St. Continue to follow E Gurley St. Turn right at Grove Avenue. Turn left at Whipple Street. Continue on Iron Springs Road. Destination will be on your right. Drive through gates. Kate will be on your left at bottom of the hill.

Yuma County

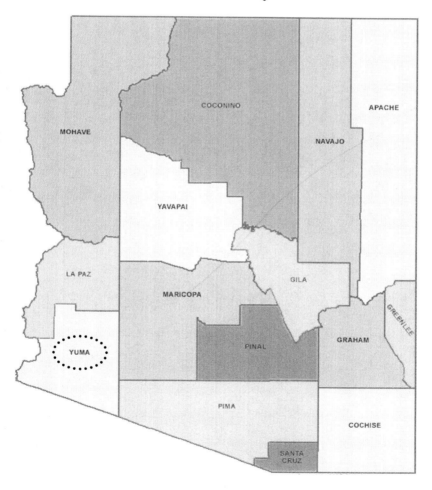

Yuma Territorial Prison Hill

An over view of the Yuma Territorial Prison Cemetery

The life of a prisoner in the Yuma Territorial Prison was not easy. There were 111 prisoner deaths during the 33 years the prison facility was open. 104 of these inmates were buried in the cemetery on the prison grounds. Seven others were claimed by their families and buried elsewhere. Only one female prisoner was interred in the prison cemetery. A convict by the name of Devaux tried to escape on the train taking him to Yuma. Unfortunately, he died when he jumped from the moving train and hit his head on a rock. He too is buried in the lonely graveyard.

Most of the deceased prisoners died from Tuberculosis (Consumption) which circulated quickly in the prison. A separate cell block was opened for these unfortunate men. Prisoners also died from accidents in the rock quarry, stabbings and homicides from fellow inmates, suicides, shot following escape attempts, and various health issues.

The prison cemetery is near the Colorado River

Burials were simple and carried out in a speedy manner. A shallow grave was dug by fellow inmates, and the wooden casket containing the dead was lowered in the ground. It was covered with the hard caliche soil and overlaid with the quarried rocks. The grave markers were constructed of wood with the prisoner's name, number and date of death. There were no mourners, no tears, and no flowers.

Stones designate the graves of the Yuma Prison inmates

The wooden markers slowly wore away from the harsh Yuma weather, termites, and souvenir hunters. By the 1950's most of the handmade tombstones were gone. The grave marker of J. F. Floyd has been recovered and on displayed in the prison museum.

The unmarked graves tell no tales

A visit to Prison Hill might spark a few EVP's if you are lucky to be visiting the cemetery in between the noise of the ongoing trains and freeway noises. One can assume these prisoners still wish to voice their strong opinions, cry out for justice, or perhaps express sorrow for their misdeeds. Some say these inmates were never paroled from this prison, even in death. A visit to the graves at Prison Hill is very eerie as the sun goes down and darkness blankets the rows of graves. You can almost hear the clanging of chains and shackles. Be sure and take some photos, you never know who might show up in the mug shot!

Directions:
From Phoenix: Take I 10 East then I 8 West. The Yuma Territorial Prison State Historical Park is located at 1 Prison Hill Road in Yuma, Arizona. Take I-8 to Yuma; take Exit 1 to Giss Parkway. Turn on Prison Hill Road.

Yuma Territorial Prison State Park
1 Prison Hill Road
Yuma, AZ 85364
928-783-4771
http://azstateparks.com/Parks/YUTE/index.html
SAVE THE YUMA TERRITORIAL PRISON
http://savetheprison.com

Tombstone Symbols

Symbol	Meaning
Anchor/Ships	Hope or Seafaring profession
Arches	Victory in Death, Being Rejoined in Heaven With Partner
Arrows	Mortality
Beehive	Domestic Virtues, Education, Faith, Abundance in the Promised Land , Piety
Bell	Mourning
Bird	Eternal Life, Winged Soul, Spirituality
Book	The Devine Word or One's Accomplishments
Bouquets/Flowers	Condolences, grief, sorrow
Broken Column	Early Death, Grief, Loss of Head of Family
Broken Ring	Family Circle Severed
Buds/Rosebud	Morning of Life or Renewal of Life
Bugles	Resurrection and the Military
Burning Flame	Life or Resurrection
Butterfly	Short-lived—Early Death, Resurrection
Candle being Snuffed	Time, mortality
Caterpillar	Life, Metamorphosis
Celtic Cross	Faith and Eternity
Chain with Three Links	Trinity, Faith, Odd Fellows
Cherub	Angelic
Coffin, Father Time, Darts, Picks/Shovels	Mortality
Column	Noble Life
Conch Shell	Wisdom, Reincarnation
Corn	Ripe Old Age
Cross	Emblem of Faith, Resurrection
Crossed Swords	High-ranking military person
Crown	Glory of Life After Death
Crown Upon Skull	Triumph of Death
Cup or Chalice	The Sacrament
Cypress	Hope
Dolphin	Resurrection, Salvation, Bearer of Souls Across Water to Heaven
Door	Entrance to Heaven
Dove	Innocence, Gentleness, Affection, Purity

Symbol	Meaning
Drapery or Pall	Mourning or Mortality
Eagle	Courage, Faith, Generosity, Contemplation, Military
Eye	Humility
Female Figure	Sorrow, Grief
Finger Pointing Downward	Calling the Earth to Witness
Finger Pointing Upward	Pathway to Heaven, Heavenly Reward
Fish	Faith, Life, Spiritual Nourishment
Flag	Military, Patriotism
Fleur De Lys	Perfection, Light, Life, Royalty
Flower	Life's Frailty, Immortality
Flying Birds	Flight of the Soul, Rebirth
Frog	Worldly Pleasure, Sin
Fruits	Eternal plenty
Full-Blown Rose	Prime of Life
Garland	Victory in death
Grim Reaper	Inevitability of Death
Gun	Military Service
Hair Flowing	Penitence
Hand of God Chopping	Sudden Death
Hands Clasped	Farewell, Hope of Meeting in Eternity
Handshakes	Farewell
Harp	Praise to the Maker, Hope
Heart	Soul in Bliss, Love of Christ, Devotion, Sorrow, Joy, Mortality
Heart Pierced By Sword	Virgin Mary, Christ, Repentance
Heart Flaming	Religious Fervor
Helmet	Military
Horns	The Resurrection
Horseshoe	Protection Against Evil
Hourglass	Swiftness of Time, Temperance
Hourglass w/Wings of Time	Time Flying/Short Life
IHS	Eternity, Christian Symbol: "In His Service
Imps	Mortality
ISIS	Rebirth, The Virgin Mary
Ivy	Friendship and Immortality
Lamb	Innocence Especially on a Childs Grave, Resurrection

Symbol	Meaning
Laurel	Fame, Victory, Triumph
Lily or Lily of Valley	Emblem of Innocence and Purity
Lion	Courage, Bravery, Strength
Lotus	Purity, Resurrection, Perfect Beauty, Spiritual Revelation
Masonic Compass and Set Square	Freemasons, Uprightness, Judgment
Memento Mori	Symbol of Death and Reminder of Mortality
Menorah	Devine Wisdom
Mistletoe	Immortality
Moon	Death, Rebirth, Victory, Sorrow of the Crucifixion
Morning Glory	Beginning of Life
Mother and Child	Charity, Love
Myrtle	Undying Love, Peace
Naked Figure	Truth, Purity, Innocence
Oak Leaves and Acorn	Maturity, Ripe Old Age
Obelisk	Rebirth, Connection Between Earth and Heaven
Olive Branch	Peace, Forgiveness, Humanity
Open Book/ Bible	Deceased Teacher, Minister, etc.
Open Gates	Afterlife, The Soul Entering Heaven
Orb	Faith
Owl	Wisdom, Solitude, A Warning of Impending Death
Pall	Mortality, Mourning
Palm Branch	Signifies Victory and Rejoicing
Pansy	Remembrance, Meditation
Pick	Death, Mortality
Poppy	Eternal Sleep
Portals	Passageway to eternal journey
Pyramid	Resurrection, Eternal Life, Enlightenment, Spiritual Attainment
Rainbow	Union, Fulfillment of the Promise of Resurrection
Ripened Fruit	Nourishment of the Soul
Rod and Staff	Comfort to the Bereaved
Rooster	Awakening, Resurrection, Courage, Vigilance
Rope Circle	Eternity

Symbol	Meaning
Roses	Victory, Pride, Triumphant Love, Purity, Brevity of earthly existence
Scallop Shell	Rebirth, Baptism, Resurrection, Life Everlasting, Pilgrimage of Life
Scarab	Resurrection, Transcendence
Scepter	Fortitude
Scythe	Death, Cutting Life Short, The Final Harvest
Severed Branch	Mortality
Shamrock	Irish Descent, Holy Trinity
Shattered Urn	Old Age
Sheaf of Wheat	Ripe for Harvest, Divine Harvest, Fruitful Life
Shells	Pilgrimage of Life
Shepherd's Crook	Charity
Skeleton	Death, Life's Brevity
Skull & Crossed Bones	Death, Crucifixion
Skull	Transitory Nature of Earthly Life, Penitence, Mortality
Sleeping Cherub	Innocence (Usually on Childs Grave)
Smoke	Vanity, Futility of Seeking Earthly Glory
Snail	Laziness, Sin
Snake, Encircled	Everlasting Life in Heaven
Spade	Mortality, Death
Spider Web	Human Frailty
Star	Devine Guidance
Star of David	Unity, Transformation
Stars and Stripes Around Eagle	Eternal Vigilance, Liberty
Steps, 3 Tiered	Faith, Hope and Charity
Sun disc, Winged	Spirituality, Everlasting Life
Sun Rising	Renewed Life, Resurrection
Sun Setting	Death
Sun shining	Everlasting Life
Swallow	Motherhood, Spirit of Children, Consolation
Sword, Broken	Life Cut Short
Sword, Inverted	Relinquishment of Power, Victory
Sword, Sheathed	Temperance
Sword	Military

Symbol	Meaning
Swords, Crossed	Life Lost in Battle
Tablets of the Decalogue	Containing the Text From Exodus and Deuteronomy given to Moses on Mount Sinai as a Symbol of the Old Covenant
Tetragrammaton	Four Hebrew Letters Y, H, W, H Spelling the True Name of God, Reminder of God's Omnipresence
Thistles	Remembrance, Scottish Descent, Earthly Sorrow
Tombs	Mortality
Torch Inverted	Life Extinguished
Torch	Immortality, Purification, Truth, Wisdom
Tree Stump w/Ivy	Head of Family—Immortality
Tree	Life, Knowledge, The Fall of Man Through sin
Tree Sprouting	Life Everlasting
Tree Stump	Life Interrupted
Tree Trunk	Brevity of Life, Number of Broken Branches Can Indicate Deceased Family Members buried at That Site
Tree Trunk Leaning	Short Interrupted Life, Mourning
Triangle	Holy Trinity
Triqueta (3 Interlocking Circles or Triangles	Eternity, Trinity, Popular Motif on Celtic Crosses
Trumpeters	Heralds of the Resurrection, Announcement of Soul's Entrance Into Heaven
Urn	Immortality, Penitence, Death of the Body and It's Return to Dust in the Final Resting Place
Urn with /Wreath or Crepe	Mourning
Urn with Blaze	Undying Friendship
Violet	Humility
Wheat	Body of Christ
Wheel	Circle of Life
Weeping Willow	Emblem of Sorrow, Mourning, Grief
Willows	Earthly Sorrow
Winged Effigies	Flight of the Soul
Winged Hourglass	Fleetness of Life, Mortality
Winged Skull	Flight of the Soul From Mortal Man

Symbol	Meaning
Wreath	Victory
Wreath of Roses	Heavenly Joy and Bliss
Wreath on Skull	Victory of Death over Life
Yin Yang Circle	Harmony, Balance, Birth and Death

The Amazing Cemetery Crawl

The Amazing Cemetery Crawl was developed in the fall of 2005 as a way for cemetery lovers to see and experience the different styles and sizes of cemeteries in Arizona. The Cemetery Crawl started as a one day excursion around the local Phoenix area cemeteries, and has now become a yearly spring weekend event that covers various historic routes across Arizona.

Part road rally, part scavenger hunt, teams are directed to a cemetery destination where they must decipher a poetic clue to find a certain tombstone in that particular cemetery. After photographing the tombstone described in the clue, the teams must present the photo to the "Cemetery Attendant" who hands them an envelope with the directions and clues to the next destination. Ah, but there are many road blocks and detours along the way to add to the fun. It is the perfect adventure for those seeking to learn the history of Arizona's and its unique cemeteries.

Here are some of the highlights of the past Cemetery Crawls. The MVD Ghostchasers invite the public to participate in future cemetery crawls by contacting Debe Branning at www.mvdghost-chasers.com

- Cemetery Crawl 1 took place in October 2005. It was a one day event that found teams dashing around the Phoenix metro area cemeteries.

- Cemetery Crawl 2 became a two day event in January 2007 and focused on central Arizona and the Prescott Valley vicinity.

- Cemetery Crawl 3 switched to April 2008 and covered Eastern Arizona with a Good Guy/Bad Man theme.

- Cemetery Crawl 4 in April 2009 headed to western Arizona and some of its Desert Rest cemeteries.

- Cemetery Crawl 5 was held in April 2010 and the teams experienced the Arizona Western section of the Mother Road Route 66.

- Cemetery Crawl 6 in April 2011 traveled into an unexpected snow storm as they traveled the Arizona Eastern section of the Mother Road Route 66.

- Cemetery Crawl 7 headed south in April 2012 and made a run to the border towns and their decorative desert cemeteries.

About the Author

Debe Branning has been the director of the MVD Ghostchasers of Mesa/Bisbee paranormal team since 1995. The team conducts investigations of haunted, historical locations throughout Arizona. For the past ten years she has lead Spirit Workshops which provides ghost hunters, paranormal team members, and folks wanting to try the art of ghost hunting a chance to work and learn techniques together. Debe has been a guest lecturer at Ottawa University, Central Arizona College, Arizona State University and South Mountain Community College. She has been a speaker at SciFi Conventions such as CopperCon, FiestaCon, HauntedCon and AZParaCon. She recently appeared in an episode of "Streets of Fear" for FearNet. com which aired October 2009 and an episode of TRAVEL CHANNEL'S "Ghost Stories" about haunted Jerome, Arizona in July 2010. Debe is the author of *Sleeping With Ghosts—A Ghost Hunter's Guide to AZ's Haunted Hotels and Inns* and two children's books. She pens a column for *Examiner.com* titled "Arizona Haunted Sites" so travelers will know where they might find a ghost or two when they visit Arizona. Debe is a REIKI Master and a dowser. Debe is currently on the Board of Directors of the Pioneers' Cemetery Association and organizes Historic Cemetery Tours for the organization.

A native of Omaha, Nebraska, Debe has resided in Mesa, Arizona for over 30 years. During this time, she has traveled to every corner of the state studying Arizona's history and culture, and enjoying haunted places along the way. In addition to traveling and writing, her hobbies include collecting celebrity dolls, genealogy, organizing ghost tours, and volunteering at the Pioneer and Military Memorial Park Cemetery in Phoenix. She is the proud parent of two children, Justin Hampton and Nicole Wheeler and is the "grammy" to Wyatt, Garrett, Louden and Gabrianna.

You can contact Debe Branning at www.mvdghostchasers.com or www.examiner.com/x-2345-Arizona-Haunted-Sites-Examiner

More Ghostly Adventures from
American Traveler Press

Sleeping With Ghosts

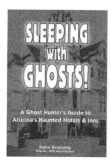

Ghostly encounters of the Arizona kind! Tour Arizona's haunted hotels, inns and bed and breakfasts. Join paranormal investigator, Debe Branning, as she relates legends and her personal experiences at Arizona's most haunted accommodations!   5 1/2 x 8 1/2 — 152 Pages . . . $12.95

Haunted Arizona
Ghosts of the Grand Canyon State

Witnesses at these haunted sites swear that the spirits of those who lived in Arizona's wild past are still among us. From ruthless outlaws to priests and Victorian ladies, these stories will amaze you! By Ellen Robson, co-author of *Haunted Highway: The Spirits of Route 66.*
5 1/2 x 8 1/2 — 136 pages . . . $12.95

Haunted Highway:
The Spirits of Route 66

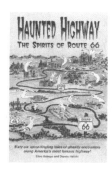

Sixty-six spine-tingling tales of haunted homes, businesses and graveyards along America's "Mother Road." From the *Biograph Theater* in Chicago to the *Pointe Vincente Lighthouse* on the Pacific Coast, these fascinating accounts of ghostly activities will provide you with hours of reading enjoyment. Take a trip on Route 66 as the authors investigate and record the stories of those with either firsthand knowledge of the ghostly legends or actual encounters. *Haunted Highway* is a great guide for the adventurous wishing to perhaps encounter one of the inhabitants of this spooky route, too. By Ellen Robson and Dianne Halicki.
5 1/2 x 8 1/2—192 Pages…$12.95

ORDER BLANK

AMERICAN TRAVELER PRESS

 5738 North Central Avenue • Phoenix, AZ 85012

www.americantravelerpress.com • 1-800-521-9221 • FAX 602-234-3062

Qty	Title	Price	Amount
	Arizona Adventure	9.95	
	Arizona Cookbook	9.95	
	Arizona Legends and Lore	9.95	
	Arizona Territory Cookbook	9.95	
	Arizona Trails and Tales	14.95	
	Arizoniana	9.95	
	Arrows, Bullets and Saddle Sores	9.95	
	Billy the Kid Cookbook	9.95	
	Cowboy Slang	9.95	
	Days of the West	14.95	
	Desert Survival Handbook	8.95	
	Discover Arizona!	6.95	
	Experience Jerome	6.95	
	Finding Gold in the Desert	5.95	
	Ghost Towns and Historical Haunts in Arizona	12.95	
	Haunted Arizona	12.95	
	Hiking Arizona	6.95	
	In Old Arizona	9.95	
	Mavericks—Ten Uncorralled Westerners	5.00	
	Old West Adventures in Arizona	9.95	
	Prehistoric Arizona	5.00	
	Sleeping with Ghosts	12.95	
	Tales of Arizona Territory	14.95	
	Wild West Heroes & Rogues: Wyatt Earp	6.95	

U.S. Shipping & Handling Add: (Shipping to all other countries see website.)	1-3 Books $3.00 4+ Books $5.00	
Arizona residents add 9.3% sales tax		

☐ My Check or Money Order Enclosed

☐ MasterCard ☐ VISA ☐ AMEX ☐ Discover

Total $ _____
(Payable in U.S. funds)

Verification code_____

Acct. No. _____ Exp. Date _____

Signature_____

Name _____ Phone _____

Address_____

City/State/Zip _____

Call for a FREE catalog of all our titles — Prices subject to change —